TACTICAL READING: A SNAPPY GUIDE TO THE SNAP GENERAL ELECTION 2017

.

TACTICAL READING:
A SNAPPY GUIDE TO THE SNAP GENERAL ELECTION 2017

EYEWEAR PUBLISHING

edited by
Alexandra Payne & Todd Swift

SQUINT
BOOKS

First published in 2017
by Eyewear Publishing Ltd
Suite 333, 19-21 Crawford Street
Marylebone, London W1H 1PJ
United Kingdom

Cover design and typeset by Edwin Smet
Printed in England by TJ International Ltd, Padstow, Cornwall

ISBN 978-1-911335-95-5

*Eyewear wishes to thank Jonathan Wonham for his
generous patronage of our press.*

The co-editors worked to a very tight schedule, but hope this
is an error-free book; any errors that crept in, of omission or
inclusion, are likely due to eye wear.

WWW.EYEWEARPUBLISHING.COM

TABLE OF CONTENTS

THE NATIONS/REGIONS

EDITORS' PREFACE

Snap elections mean one thing for publishers, above all else – not much time to get a book out. This one was announced six weeks before 8th June, and we will only be at the printers by the second week of May. So why do it? Well, Eyewear, as a British indie press has a history of doing politically-timely non-fiction books in this series, Squint. In the past two years, we predicted the elections of Corbyn, and Trump – but also published books on Clinton and Sanders (among others). We wanted to contribute, in a modest way, to the debates happening.

And this book will have time to make an impact – because it only takes a few hours to read it and you will have weeks to get a copy into the hands of your friends, family, neighbours, co-workers, and lovers; even if you bought it on June 8th, it could change your mind.

The most vital thing about this book is that, for the most part, its snapshot, side-eye look at all the main parties, the regions, and the key issues, is written by people way outside of the Westminster bubble – and its views are not those, for the most part, of pundits, talking heads, and the usual journos – probably perfectly nice people, but often so close they can't see the wood for the trees.

The media in the UK is especially bad at being objective about polls, polling, and the chances of, say,

Corbyn or the Lib Dems doing well. Given that Corbyn won after being a 200-1 long shot; and given what we know about the disastrous ability to connect polling to democratic outcomes for Trump and the last UK election, it seems fair to say that we still do not know, even with only weeks to go, exactly what will happen. Yet the media wants us to think it is pretty much a done deal.

By presenting a snappy guide like this, written by an NHS cleaner, teachers, former armed forces personnel, poets, mums, dads – concerned voters – what might be called 'ordinary people' (except for maybe the poets) – get to make their voices heard. However, there are also some 'experts' here because who's to say that anyone's viewpoint is useless at a time like this?

Well, it is an odd time. Where the rest of the world seems vibrantly off-kilter, with sweeping changes and screw-you-all voting tactics, the British, perhaps stultified by a conservative press, or a sense of low-level despair, don't seem possessed (after their Brexit vote) to upset any apple carts. The voters of the UK have the chance to weaken or dispose of a Tory mandate to bring in a hard Brexit, but they seem disengaged from the idea of a Corbynite or Lib Dem revolution.

It could be a coronation for Mrs May, who promises to be 'bloody difficult' indeed regarding the EU. This book argues there is much still to play for – at the local electoral level, where many contests are still open to tactical voting, or genuine wins, for the Greens, Labour, and Lib Dems, as well as the SNP and parties in Northern Ireland and Wales, who would do their best to slow the pace of a drastic Brexit decision.

If you are like us, you probably are a bit tired of the B-word – Brexit is an ugly word (if not an ugly concept) – but this election is not about the economy, or jobs, or education or the NHS, really.

Nor is it really about leadership, or avoiding chaos, or national unity. It is really about where you as a voter stand on the most important issue in the UK and Europe this year – and likely for the next five – how the UK will leave its deeply-entrenched union with 27 other nations it counts as trading partners and peaceful allies. Forget how May eats fish and chips, or how often Tim Farron smells your spaniel; or how many errors Diane Abbott makes on the radio. Or even if Corbyn has shaved his beard, or knotted his tie properly.

The question is probably, where do they stand on Brexit? And, we know the Lib Dems will offer some kind of a second referendum on any deal Europe (likely to be belligerent) offers; the Tories are playing hardball, holding out for a hard Brexit, or bust. Labour is a bit less clear, arguably, on where it stands… and then the smaller parties, and those in Wales, Northern Ireland, and Scotland, are lining up to offer their own particular flavours and slants on the whole messy process.

It would be a shame if, at such a divided and confused time, the voters of Britain played it entirely safe, and did not instead vote tactically, intelligently, and with their consciences, risking much to potentially surprise many and make something extraordinary occur. Polls lie. Some news may be faked. Only one thing seems true, even at this late stage – no one is actually elected to power until after all the ballots have been cast, and then honestly counted. Fasten your seatbelts. The battle bus is speeding, and it may have lying posters on its sides…

Editors' note on the recent by-elections:
Warnings about assuming that local election results will be reflected in a General Election are widespread and perfectly wise. But this is not normal timing; council seats are hardly ever contested mere weeks before parliamentary seats. The headline figures for the Conservatives were very encouraging: they made hundreds of gains, with UKIP voters jumping directly to them and the Lib Dems stumbling even in key parts of the UK. And while Labour could point to some decent results in Wales, they had a torrid time, losing hundreds of councillors elsewhere. There is a clear swing to the Tories, and so for supporters of the other parties, the need to get the vote out and try harder must clearly be redoubled.

The editors, Alexandra Payne & Todd Swift
8 May, 2017

INTRODUCTION: WHAT ARE VOTERS THINKING?

by Nik Nanos

Some called these events unfathomable: Trump winning the American Presidency and the Brexit forces edging out the pro-European Union establishment in the United Kingdom. Both outcomes shattered popular wisdom and blindsided the establishment. What do these events have in common? On the one side were the fist-pumping victors, happy that the message of angry discontent was sent. On the other side were the chest-clutching vanquished, disbelieving results that seem void of rationality. There was little room in between.

The twist in the story is the tyranny of small swings in voter sentiment: how very small voter swings have disproportionate impact on the shape and type of governments. It does not take many angry or anxious voters to influence democratic outcomes and the types of parties and leaders that win elections. For example, in the case of US President Donald Trump, a swing of one voter in 2,500 in the right states tipped the balance in his favour in the Electoral College outcome. The lesson here is that one should not confuse the views of elected governments with the views of citizens. The Trump victory was a slim mathematical probability, driven not just by anti-establishment anger but also by a rejection of Clinton as the candidate of the Washington elites. In that sense, Trump was also an instrument to punish the establishment, not just a rallying point for his views.

The populist anger is anti-establishment in tone and economic in foundation and it divides nations along educational lines rather than by income, as seen in the UK Brexit vote and US presidential vote. This is not classic class warfare between high and low income voters. This is war between those of high education attainment and those of lower education attainment, with low-attainment voters feeling marginalized, at risk and immersed in a mindset of declinism – in which nations and neighbourhoods are believed to be on the decline and the future for citizens and their children lack optimism.

I would argue that the aggregation of political choices by voters is being influenced by very small swings of angry voters, and that politicians catering to those angry voters govern to feed their angry coalition. Elections, which are the aggregation of political choices by voters within a set of institutional rules, are ideally the democratic expression of the will of the people. Hopefully this aggregation produces a social good that is reflective of that will. Election outcomes and the governing style of the angry and the interpretations we bring to them are being influenced by very small swings of angry voters. It is the tail wagging the dog.

In a world of economic uncertainty, the margins and the marginalised are shaping political dialogue and election outcomes. In this world, governments seem stable but they are not – they are actually quite vulnerable to small swings in opinion. One could argue that many elections are influenced by small swings but an examination of recent votes suggests that the emerging angry populist politics is something qualitatively different both in terms of impact and the anti-establishment style of politicians. With these small swings, stability is a misnomer when applied to a government that governs for years based on a public-opinion snapshot on election day.

For the Trump win and the Brexit vote, what really happened? One could argue that this is part of a widespread populist uprising against the establishment – that voters are rising up in anger. However, a look at the numbers and the environment suggests something different. Voter anger exists, but not all of the people who voted for Trump, or Brexit can be characterised by a populist uprising. The activation of this anger, however, is having a disproportionate impact on democratic outcomes. These are not mass movements – they are micro movements with mass impact fuelled by anger. Think of the math the way strategists and politicians do, as they strive to calculate a winning strategy.

Winning an election in a two-way race can be a daunting undertaking. Not so when one breaks down the political challenge from a mathematical perspective. Assume Party X is four per centage points ahead of Party Y in a national election. Strictly by the numbers, the trailing party has to merely persuade a paltry one citizen in 20 to switch their vote to turn the defeat into a victory. A change of five percentage points in the preferences of voters has a net 10-point impact on the election race and yields a different outcome.

One should not think of an election as a mass rejection or embrace of a politician. In fact, it is more a micro rejection or embrace. The key point is that from a mathematical perspective, in many cases only a handful of voters truly decide the outcome of an election. With this in mind, politicians riding this wave of anger should not confuse the small swings that put them in power with the views of the citizens writ large.

The traditional way of conceptualising voters, as rational actors, imagines them evaluating, judging, poking and prodding the policies and leadership styles of politicians, searching out a good choice that makes sense. One could be an economic voter, calculating their personal gain and the direct impact of the campaign promises of the choices before them. Alternatively, a citizen could be a leadership-driven voter, looking for the personality that is best suited to lead. Some voters even cast their ballot against their personal self-interest. They are selfless voters. For example, the champagne socialist is ready to vote for the politician promising to impose higher taxes on the rich – and willing to vote against their personal economic interest for the sake of the social contract that binds society. The poor need help; the rich quite simply can and should pay. Parties like voters who are true believers – left wing, right wing, nationalists, globalists, environmentalists – bound by an unshakable ideological faith and looking for politicians who share their beliefs. These are many of the traditional ways to think of voters. They share a sense of rationality, whether it be ideological or economic in the sense that the political choice is expected to align with a particular set of outcomes. More importantly, in these conceptions, democracy enables solutions rather than being the problem.

The Trump win in the US and the Brexit victory have a different dimension, the dimension of anger. Some voters believe not just that politicians have failed citizens but that the system itself is failing citizens. The 'lock her up' chants at Trump rallies, aimed at Democratic nominee Hillary Clinton, were about Trump supporters believing that the system had failed and that punishment was required. She happened to be Trump's opponent and the embodiment of the Washington establishment which, Trump supporters believed, had failed America. The key takeaway is that the neat and tidy view of the rational voter inadequately captures the reality of the angry voter who is more emotional.

Add to this the phenomenon of social media as a public but anonymous space for angry voters, and the minority now have a platform to vent. Democratic dialogue is being reshaped through social media services such as Twitter, 140 characters at time, in a post-truth world where the facts can be less influential on democratic outcomes than emotions. Angry voters are nothing new. However, the wildfire rapidity of angry voter sentiment, ignited by politicians, propelled by social media and charged with emotion, presents a new twist on democratic dialogue.

The creation, propagation and use of mistruths and misinformation as part of the democratic dialogue further fuels the anger and adds a dimension of irrationality. Fake news, fabricated information, truth-deniers enabled by the World Wide Web and social media further enable the angry mindset.

In this world, lies are cheaper than the truth. Engaging in a policy debate on substantive issues is expensive and for some voters, perhaps, too onerous. The shorthand of convenient facts and symbolic politics where promises do not have to be literally true is a product of the new high velocity political age. It is true that many political battles in the past were also symbolic. The new political fuzziness of the truth propelled by the Internet and social media brings to mind the dystopian future of George Orwell. Here, Donald Trump is an example of rule by demagogic fiat enabled by Twitter and his followers.

In effect, one should not ask 'what were voters thinking?' but 'why weren't leaders listening?' Not only have the rules of the game changed, but the game itself.

Nik Nanos, the founder and Executive Chairman of Nanos Research, is one of the world's leading pollsters and business strategists. A former National President of the Marketing Research and Intelligence Association his is the official pollster for CTV News, and leads one of Can-

ada's most distinguished research companies. He is a Global Fellow at the Woodrow Wilson International Centre for Scholars in Washington DC and a research associate professor at the State University of New York at Buffalo.

CUTTING THROUGH THE PROPHECIES

by Annie Alsen

In a poll recently conducted of 2,000 low-income registered voters, approximately 47% stated it was highly likely that 'Landslide' is Fleetwood Mac's best song. No wait, was it that Theresa May is likely to win in a landslide? Sorry, it's hard to remember where you stand in general election coverage these days. It might have been that Corbyn has halved the Tory lead? Or that the Liberal Democrats stand a chance again? Or that John Bercow has finally melted into a ball of hot magma after the latest round of ministerial indiscretions? The only thing we can be sure of is that 'Gold Dust Woman' is the best thing to have ever been dragged from Stevie Nicks' guts.

Think back to 2015. A year described by historians as 'culturally similar to vanilla yoghurt' and '*only* two years ago?' The polls said we were headed for another hung parliament. A Guardian/ICM poll had Labour and the Conservatives on 35% of the vote each. Another hung parliament for the UK it seemed. A coalition deal was to be struck and the future looked divided. Most of the media coverage was herding the alternative factoid rumours that Labour looked to the burgeoning SNP as their coalition partners. Everywhere you went, people said it was 'too early to tell', as if the future of the United Kingdom had suddenly turned into the painful dream-space between stubbing your toe and knowing if you've broken it or not. This air of unease is difficult to allay in voting and eventually it did teeter down on the side of a Conservative majority and an SNP power-house in Scotland – a majority that some would argue has more to do with the safety of incumbency than it does in how well the Tories presented themselves in the run-up to the election. The polls predicted uncertainty and the voters gave them the opposite.

Then the following year, we found ourselves in the midst of a referendum. A Populus poll conducted on the 22nd May, the day before the vote, placed the Remain camp at 55% of the vote and Leave at 45%; a prediction that had been continuing somewhat since the announcement. Most media outlets had suggested a Remain win. Former UKIP leader and human quotation mark Nigel Farage, one of the strongest Leave supporters, stated at the time 'Remain would edge it'. We know now that the result would blow people's minds in a way that divided the left and right brain hemispheres. But it's obviously got a lot to do with where you get your media. My social media bubble was mainly Remain voters with a few Leave voters sprinkled in. I thought: if everyone I know is saying the same as me, it must be pretty likely. In fact, out of the 130 independent EU referendum polls that I could be bothered to Google, only 50 predicted a Leave result. Nearly 1 in 3. Polling data takes small samples of different populations, which if you compare the polls, would have emphasised a greater chance at a Leave win.

Most media groups kept their bubbles to fit their editorial standpoint, and there is confirmation bias in this as well. If you sample a population of your own readers in your polls, they're going to agree with you on what the best kind of quinoa is, and the bigger the bubble, the greater the amplification of those voices. The print and broadcast media predicted certainty and the voters gave them the opposite.

So where are we in 2017? At the time of writing, a YouGov poll conducted for the *Times* has the Conservatives on 45%, Labour on 29%, the Liberal Democrats at 10%, UKIP at 7% of the vote and the SNP retaining the 5% they will need to hold on to Scotland. Various polls are predicting similar figures with most stating that the gulf between the Tories and Labour is narrowing to indicate another very close race. My social media feed is awash with: 'Corbyn, that manhole cover guy, is correct on housing' and 'Farron: probably not Nick Clegg/an egg salad sandwich' – and I'm starting to think that the polls narrowing means we're in for a Tory supermajority. After all, the polls are predicting closeness, so the voters will give us the opposite, right? Or – perhaps more scarily – the same result as the last vote: a damning indictment that the country is perhaps relatively happy with how things have been going in the wake of Article 8 and a sudden increased reliance on charities and food banks. So, do we believe in these self-fulfilling (literally) prophecies – by existing, are they proving the contrary of what they are predicting?

Well, not necessarily. Everyone knows

that guy in the pub who swears betting odds are the only way to accurately gauge how people will vote. Admittedly, he is the same guy that believes John Lennon drives the 905 National Express from Woking to Heathrow. But there is good reasoning there: people generally do put their money where their mouth is. Tabloid fish-tank cleaner *The Mirror* recently reminded us that 'all major bookmakers make the Tories heavy odds-on favourites to win both the most seats and an overall majority.' The odds for the Leave campaign winning the EU referendum dramatically lengthened in the run-up to the vote and in 2010, some betting markets advised that no single party would win a majority. But then it makes some sense, if capital is just a strong idea, and therefore an economy is a marketplace of strong ideas, there is literally no difference between betting and opinion polling. There is obviously so much at stake in a general election, but people's valuations of this stake will always differ.

Let's get down to brass tacks. This is early doors. The manifestos are still arriving, the rosettes are still unfurling. Only about five Labour backbenchers have had their annual coat of Ronseal. Where can the polls go? Can Jeremy Corbyn lead Labour to power? Well, the percentages aren't looking good. In fact, in most polls, Labour is bobbing around the mid-20s at the moment – a number that if repeated at the general election by a solemn Andrew Mc-

Neil would be Labour's worst result ever. Labour haven't polled above 30% in months. And it's not as if Jeremy has the 'Big Mo' behind him – that is to say: Bob Ainsworth. If you're out for a Labour majority in this snap election, you better hope that – as almost always – the opinion polls are wrong.

So the polls aren't for you. We've established that. You're not keen on the market either. So which predictions will see you through from the shiny French tips of April to the raw nail-beds of June? Your bubble, of course! Bending your mind back to the last year in which you honestly weren't asleep during the rise of a tiny-handed despotic potato (see also: dict-ato), the Trump campaign were greatly lagging behind in the polls. The markets didn't predict Trump, despite having birthed him fully clothed and at the age of 47 some years before. Social media predicted Trump.

No one really knows how influential sharing politics on social media is. Does a like mean a vote? Does a retweet? 4cinsights.com, in their post-match analysis, found Trump had consistently higher positive sentiment shown towards him on social media than Clinton did. Social media found the gap that traditional polling missed: that you are more truthful to your friends than the poll guy calling you at 8pm to ask about politics when you've got Thai ordered and are trying to get through the latest episode of *Line of Duty*. According to research conducted by Vyacheslav Polonski concerning the EU referendum, 'social media data analysis shows that not only did Brexit supporters have a more powerful and emotional message, but they were also more effective in the use of social media.'

People simply trust their peers in a way that they don't trust huge institutions. How can you believe the polling data, the market data or endorsements from the private sector in a world of alternative facts? Even some politicians worry over the integrity of institutional prophecy: French presidential candidate and William Devane lookalike Jean Lassalle stated to *Le Figaro*: 'Even if I would transform water into wine, the polls would continue to place me at 0.5 per cent.' People get polling data from the media rather than directly from the website. According to the Edelman Trust Barometer, 43% of Brits stated they trust the media – a drop from 51% the year before. And would you believe I got that titbit of info from a *Financial Times* report. This is *Inception*-level mind fog – the media supports the polls, people distrust the media, ergo they distrust the polls – and it's not hard to figure out that the totem lands on the side of social media bubbles. A report from the Media Insight Project in 2015 showed that Facebook is most people's main source of information regarding culture, sport and most importantly, social issues.

These social issues are usually protest issues, largely falling towards mistrust of the government at the time – something which the polls occasionally reflect. But social media, probably in similar regard to the print media, reflects poorly on the opposition parties too. As Isaac Newton didn't say: to every criticism of the government's austerity policy, there is an equal and opposite big red bus. Social media casts a wide shadow – and whilst it is true that it allows people of similar political affiliations to find each other and share ideas, like all bubbles, it promulgates insularity and widens the gulf between political positions.

Most people called the GE 2015 'the first social media campaign' – because, as everyone knows, Michael Howard's Bebo account was just Hawthorne Heights lyrics and oversaturated polaroids of John Major wearing aviators. Everything suddenly became meme-able. I personally have watched 112 remix videos of Ed Miliband getting hit by an egg in Southampton. In terms of social media engagement during this time, the Conservative Party recorded more likes on their Facebook page than the Labour party, but they also didn't have to do very much in order to make presentation more important than policies. They just pointed the finger at a guy eating a bacon sandwich and said 'that guy can't even handle meat and bread. What a lunatic'.

There's a saying I've invented for this now. For when you re-post the funny mick-take of a politician in lieu of what they're saying on housing, jobs and finance. 'Share it once, shame on you. Share it again, shame on me. And also shame on you. And shame also on Mark Zuckerberg and whomever invented Twitter (the bird, right?)'.

This is the brand new political culture. The exit polls mesmerise the tracking polls. The social media bubbles burst when people go 'I had no idea someone other than me, my dog, my postman and my friends was voting'. The media blame the polls for the result of their reinforcing that the polls could be wrong. I don't know who the polls blame – raw data? They should be blaming the common denominator – the people who ask for change or stability and then go to the polls and hand themselves the opposite. It's 2017, go find something unedited, or un-reblogged, un-shared or un-filtered on Instagram, un-sifted through the hands of the press, un-sifted through the market. And when you fail, remember when you're watching the next few months of non-stop coverage on what the polls are saying, what the markets are saying, what social media is saying – remember that you're watching speculation, not certainty. Nothing is written in stone until Theresa May engraves her name on to her own heart on June 8th. Whatever your affiliation, remember that you can go out and deliver the opposite to what you've been told. A single vote in the hands of someone thinking clearly about the difference between what they've been told and what they know is the most powerful thing in a modern democracy.

Annie Alsen is a writer from the West Country. She has been published in various magazines and journals across the United Kingdom and the United States. She currently lives in the South East.

THE
PARTIES

THERESA MAY: CITIZEN OF WHERE EXACTLY?

by Christopher Jackson

We had no time to dwell on the Easter weekend.

Tuesday morning broke, and soon the typical website-goer in the United Kingdom began to receive unusual intimations: an announcement was due from outside the door of Downing Street. It was then that the question of the day – 'Why?' – began drifting through Westminster and, via the Twitter account of Laura Kuenssberg, out into the wider country. Was Prime Minister Theresa May, a known type II diabetes sufferer, and 60 years old, about to resign? Had we somehow gone to war *again*? Or – *or* – was there to be a surprise election? On the last point, there were persuasive reasons to think not. There had, for instance, been numerous previous denials from the prime minister herself, most notably in September 2016 on The Andrew Marr Show:

> I'm not going to be calling a snap election. I've been very clear that I think we need that period of time, that stability, to be able to deal with the issues that the country is facing and have that election in 2020.[1]

May's office had also released a statement a few weeks before the Easter weekend stating that the prime min-

---

1 Quoted in 'A flashback to all the times Theresa May said a snap election was a terrible idea because it would cause 'instability'', published in *The New Statesman*, April 2017.

ister would not be calling a vote, with a Downing Street source quoted as saying 'it's not something she plans or wishes to do'[2].

To reinstate the theatrical in politics one must simply surprise journalists. These remembered denials began to feel hollow on 18th April, as the media – huddled in their insectoid camera-scrum outside Downing Street – noticed that the prime ministerial crest was not displayed on the lectern. This was a sign that what would ensue pertained to party and not government business.

And then, wrong-footing everyone again, May walked out of No. 10 Downing Street 15 minutes earlier than expected. She looked, as always, like someone on her way to somewhere else. The cameras twitched; the microphones jostled. May was brisk:

> I have just chaired a meeting of the cabinet, where we agreed that the government should call a general election, to be held on the eighth of June. I want to explain the reasons for that decision, what will happen next and the choice facing the British people when you come to vote in this election.

There it was then: May stood before us, the product of hard work and chance, and sought to ratify the accident of her rise to power. What ensued was business-like, which is to say it was the opposite of

2 M. Weaver, 'The many times Theresa May ruled out a general election', published in *The Guardian*, Tuesday 18th April 2017.

poetry. May's public addresses are reminiscent of someone pausing in the street to tell you the time. One would wish to praise their compression if the language weren't – as a character says in the US sitcom *Veep* – 'noise-shaped air'[3]. But it was the great British philosopher of language JL Austin who observed that we use language to do, as well as to assert. This was the apotheosis of that theory – words as close to deed as possible.

Even so, it was impossible not to lament the poetry deficit. As May detailed her approach to Europe, there would be no rallying cry: the nation was instead asked to partake in the logic of her premiership thus far. The referendum result. The necessity of honouring it. The failure of the Westminster parties, including her own, to be as cooperative as she might have wished. The words amassed with the mercilessness of someone who has seized a microphone at a wedding. Except that here a demand was made on listeners: to accommodate her decision to hold this election into their own lives, and vote – and perhaps vote for her.

And straightaway, the world began asking: 'Why is this happening now?' This in turn implied a subsidiary question: 'Do we need to do this at all?'

WHO IS THERESA MAY?

So why did a woman so newly installed in the prime ministership – who had repeatedly, and adamantly

---

3 The line is spoken by Dan Egan in Season Four, Episode 1.

stated that she wouldn't countenance this state of affairs – decide to opt for this route? What does she hope to gain by it? The answer to these questions is intimately linked to the identity of the woman who made the announcement.

As the nation watched this speech, it was confronted again with this inscrutable person who rules over us: one would have to go back to Clement Attlee to find a more private leader. We are not even able to say whether this remoteness is a function of shyness or calculation. Perhaps it is also inherent in the modern incarnation of the prime ministerial office: behind their microphones, cruising through the major cities of the world in their dark-windowed limousines, our leaders can seem Big Brotherish in their ubiquity and in their intentional illegibility. May is no different. Her distance from us is compounded by the language she uses, the straitened vocabulary she inhabits. It is also added to by the obscurity of her backstory. We have never known her, and now we are asked to endorse this person we do not know.

But sometimes, by a speechwriter's negligence, or simply because human beings – even those dedicated to bland utterance – are irrepressible and continually interesting in spite of their attempts not to be, a professional politician will say something suggestive. Watching May call this election it was possible to remember another speech delivered at the 2016 Conservative Party Conference, when May had strayed into the genuinely revealing:

But today, too many people in positions of power behave as though they have more in common with international elites than with the people down the road, the people they employ, the people they pass in the street. If you believe you're a citizen of the world, you're a citizen of nowhere. You don't understand what the very word 'citizenship' means.[4]

This phrase 'citizen of nowhere' has been widely claimed as a stern rebuke to Remainers – or in that tedious label so rife in the right-wing press, Remoaners. But to do May justice, it must be said that the phrase in its right context is not a taunt to those who still think it would have been preferable to remain in the European Union, so much as an exhibition of Anglican teacherliness: it is a moment of finger-wagging by May the communitarian. If it weren't for the politics of it all – which we shall come onto in a moment – one might wonder whether the reinstallation of a sense of community is what is primarily at stake in this election from May's perspective. She wants us all to be citizens of a country populated with people more akin to Theresa May. So again, the political keeps coming down to the personal: it all depends on who exactly she is.

Alarmingly, we still know little. The vicar's daughter from Eastbourne who spent the majority of her youth in Oxfordshire, grew up an only child in a household of quiet but insistent morality. Hubert Brasier, May's father, was committed to the

4 T. May, conference speech, 2016.

welfare of the community: as he made the rounds of his parish, performing the duties of a dedicated clergyman, it is not difficult to imagine the young May taking note.

May springs out of a particular idea of England, about which the worst that could be said is that it is too much austerely proud to be itself, and not some other less blessed country. It is an England of cricket and automatic Conservative Party membership, of dutiful (and far from ecstatic) attendance of the Sunday church service, and a welter of duties which should sound too clichéd to be real. These would include making a cake for the village fête, handing out leaflets at local elections *and* general elections, and even the propagation of certain character traits – modesty, propriety, hard work, thrift, all bound up in the assertion-by-example of an Anglican morality. Such traits, admirable in themselves, each have their flipsides: modesty might shade into blandness; propriety can easily turn judgmental and reduce the nation's portion of inspiration and vitality; glorying in the importance of hard work can sometimes lead to the scapegoating of the poor as 'lazy'; thrift can lead to ungenerosity; and membership of the Church of England – a national church, after all – can also tilt into a genteel xenophobia toward the Other, whether that be other branches of the Christian faith, or adherents of other religions.

May's career is a tale of clinging with surprising tenacity to this view of life. True, she has made her compromises – but she has taken care to make them quietly. Her accommodations with the government of David Cameron strike one in retrospect as having been largely to do with holding her nose whenever George Osborne made a budget. Her own administration has shown itself eager to place a different emphasis than Cameron's did on the desirability of a grammar school education, one of May's pet ideas. She has also hinted from time to time that she would be happier cutting overseas spending on international development – though she has been frightened off that particular pledge this time around, perhaps on account of Bill Gates' vocal disapproval of the idea. That leaves a lot of overlap with the Cameron administration.

Even so, May's time in the Home Office from 2010 until her elevation to the prime ministership in that astonishing summer of 2016, can be understood as a quiet assertion of her idea of England. May ran 2 Marsham Street as a department apart – a fiefdom committed to the promotion of her own values. Some of this was to the good: she brokered a deal between the UK and Jordan sealing the extradition of the unlovely Abu Hamza, whose departure from this island few would lament. Meanwhile, her cuts to the police force didn't lead to any dramatic increase in crime – or if they did, that rise hasn't yet shown itself in the official statistics. At the same time, she also lectured the Police Federation that their bad practice was not 'confined to a few bad apples': on this occasion, her High Church warnings to the profession to do its duty didn't seem wholly out of place in light of police malpractice in the Stephen Lawrence and Hillsborough affairs. Most notably, her Gladstonenian side also gave us her own proudest achievement – the Modern Slavery Act, a genuinely landmark piece of legislation which she hopes to build on in the future should she win this election.

On the other hand, May's instincts can appear throwback. At the Home Office, May also railed regularly against the immigration numbers – but always to little effect. Her frustration could lead her into blunders such as the Go Home buses episode, that surreal pilot scheme introduced to deter immigrants from remaining in the UK, which was swiftly withdrawn. It was an attempt to pull one back for Little England, and it may not be a small point that May cannot long endure the ridicule the buses engendered. Under fire, she tends to hide – if hiding doesn't work, she U-turns. If we add May's commitment to education by selection, her espousal of Trident, and her indifference to climate change, she can seem a curious person to be leading a modern country: her positions tend to reinforce the impression that May – like her adversary Jeremy Corbyn – is somewhat out of time, a creature of the 1980s, or even of the 1950s. This election has an undeniably retro feel – it's an argument over two competing visions of the past.

But her time as home secretary, suggestive though it is, has already ceded to her prime ministership. And it already seems likely, barring some other calamity, that where Blair will always be known for

Iraq – and Cameron for the European referendum –
May will be known to history for delivering the em-
barrassing buzzword portmanteau noun of the age,
which as she has always said, means itself.

BREXIT AND THIS ELECTION

'Brexit means Brexit'. That grimly epochal phrase –
as idiotic as it is pragmatic – has become strangely
inwoven in our lives. It is another indication of the
way in which, in May's world, words are always sub-
ordinate to action – in this case, the phrase can only
ever be allotted meaning by the course of events.

What is May's attitude to Europe? Again –
and again, frustratingly – we still know more about
her attitude to the EU from her time as home secretary: as prime minister, with the excuse of needing to
keep her cards close to her chest for the purposes of
the upcoming negotiation, she has given little away
beyond her desire to enact the result of the referendum, and to shoot one fine day for a quasi-mystical
Great Repeal Bill. But during the coalition years,
May would occasionally pop a Eurosceptic head
above the parapet to remind the right wing of her
party of her disapproval of the Human Rights Act,
and reiterate her wish to see that legislation scrapped.
Here is a much-derided passage from her speech to
the Conservative Party Conference in 2011:

> We all know the stories about the Human Rights
> Act... about the illegal immigrant who cannot be de-

ported because, and I am not making this up, he had a pet cat.[5]

This is May in tribal mode, and we might note in passing the tension in that 'I am not making this up'. When May strays beyond her natural seriousness into humour she must fall back on exaggeration: this can never be funny because it cannot be based on the truth where comedy is found. On this occasion, her information turned out to be false. The Judicial Office, having looked into the matter, returned with the verdict that she had misrepresented the case she had been referring to. Kenneth Clarke – that noted Remainer – was typically blunt, calling the claim 'childish'.

However, May is a different politician when she has decisions to make: as home secretary, she arrived at a more nuanced position when it came to the question of whether to opt back into the European Arrest Warrant. This warrant is operative across all European member states: once it is issued, it requires the relevant state to arrest and detain the individual in question. It is considered by most people as a useful tool of enforcement in an era of international crime. But Jacob Rees-Mogg, who called the warrant 'an important stepping stone towards a single European criminal law'[6], and the Fair Trials International are among those who argue that the system

5 Theresa May's 2011 conference speech, delivered 4th October 2011.

6 G. Heffer, 'Tory MP: Remaining in EU will see Brussels handed control of our criminal courts' published in *The Express*, May 17th 2016

can lead to injustice: for instance, there are instances where warrants have been issued years after the alleged crime, and episodes of police brutality have also been recorded. In this matter, May showed her authoritarian side. Charged with opting back into the warrant after the 2007 Lisbon Treaty, May sought to bypass parliament over the issue: her mistake here, by her own admission on Desert Island Discs a few weeks later, was to misjudge the mood of the chamber. And yet this matter also shows her not scrapping a piece of EU legislation she believes in just for the sake of it: it is another side to May – the pragmatist who, one quietly hopes, would not form a UKIP-style administration if elected in 2017.

May's idealism is usually trumped in the end by acceptance of how the world is. The ideals of a pragmatist, thin as they might eventually prove, are nevertheless likely to be deeply cherished by their possessor since they have fought their way up against the natural grain of being: perhaps she is only now preparing to reveal them. If so, it's been a long time coming: May's career can at times seem like the story of their suppression. When Cameron called his 2016 referendum, May did very little. In that giddy midsummer of 2016, she was fortunate in that her secretive instincts aligned perfectly with the strategy needed to win the leadership: while everyone else – Michael Gove, Boris Johnson et al. – manoeuvred, May understood that it was not a time for hyperactivity. Sometimes a single right decision is enough to assume considerable power. May, though only nominally a Remainer, would never have done something so radical as to trigger Article 50 without the implications of that surprise vote behind her. May isn't entirely free of principle when compared to a man like Boris Johnson, but the impression remains that there are few positions which she won't countenance provided enough people agree with them: 'Those are my principles. If you don't like them, I have others', as Groucho Marx marvellously put it. When the cause of Gary McKinnon became of interest to celebrities, she refused his extradition; when the Go Home buses proved unpopular she retired the scheme. Margaret Thatcher, with whom May is forever destined to be compared, used to call this followership not leadership.

Since her elevation May has shed her Remain garb: it is startling how comfortable she now seems in the Brexit camp – perhaps her time of real discomfort was as a tight-lipped Remainer during that 2016 referendum campaign. Faced with an exceedingly narrow 52-48 per cent vote, May – exhibiting a gumption that can still make one pause at unrelated tasks with remembered astonishment – has enacted with ruthless logic the wishes of the 52 per cent. It is hard to escape the impression that she has been, to put it kindly, somewhat unminding of the views of the 48. The question in this election is how many of those who voted Remain are silently stewing, and whether they can mobilise behind any viable strategy.

The polls show May with huge leads. A survey conducted by Survation in September 2016 showed Corbyn over 60 points less popular than Theresa May, with the prime minister enjoying a net favourability rating among voters of +33.6, while the Labour leader found himself on -30.7. That narrative hasn't really changed since that poll: it feels locked in both by Corbyn's unassuming approach to the rowdiness of politics, and by a print media predominantly favourable to the Conservatives. The numbers in late April 2017 still show Labour consistently trailing the Conservatives, usually by around 25 points.[7] You have to go back to the heyday of Blair to find an incumbent in a comparably promising situation in the lead-up to an election.

There is this faint hope for Corbynistas. Post-Trump, post-Brexit, we inhabit the age of the discredited pollster. Furthermore, there is electoral instability in the air: all the recent elections – both here and in the US – are illustrative of a fickle rage in which the disenfranchised protest whoever happens to be the incumbent party. If Corbyn can speak to those people, and tap into that well of discontent, anything is possible. Even an apparent shoo-in like May is, given today's electorate, not so much of a shoo-in as perhaps she'd like.

And yet the most probable outcome is that Theresa May will win this election.

---

7 A recent analysis by Professor John Curtice suggested that Labour might be left with as few as 190 seats if a General Election were held today.

IN THE LIKELY EVENT THAT SHE WINS

There are those who think May has called this vote in order to rid herself of certain right-wing elements within her party – those with whom, the argument runs, she had to make an uneasy accommodation at the outset of her premiership, weakened by the lack of the mandate she is now seeking. And indeed one can imagine the likes of Andrea Leadsom, her one-time rival for the job, and even Liz Truss heading out the door should she win. And yet, toxically unpopular though he is, this author finds it hard to disregard Tony Blair, writing in the *Evening Standard*:

> Some say it is to defeat the Tory Right so that she can go for a 'softer Brexit'. This is naive. The opposite is true. At present, if she wanted to face down the Tory Right she has a Parliament with a majority to do so. What she doesn't have is a Parliament that would vote for Brexit at any cost.[8]

One recalls that image of May walking hand in hand with President Donald Trump at the White House. May is not uncomfortable with the far right: it's the neoliberals, as exemplified by George Osborne, who she can't abide. And during the first chapter of her premiership she has plainly felt constrained by the 2015 Cameron manifesto.

But free of Europe, what nation would she seek to create?

---

8 T. Blair, Don't just give Theresa May the free hand she is seeking over Brexit' published in *The Evening Standard*, 21ˢᵗ April 2017.

On the economy, May is caught between wishing to help the just about managing (or the JAMs as they have become known), and her worry about how that would go down with her corporate donor base – people, in other words, from the same milieu as her banker husband Philip. May wanted to raise National Insurance on the self-employed but decided against it. On 21st April 2017, there were headlines that Philip Hammond would raise VAT, but these rumours were quickly scotched. She had plans to raise the legal fees in relation to probates – the so-called stealth death tax – but quietly dropped them also.

But Osborne's neoliberal economy – happy to trade, for instance, with a China cavalier about human rights – is, in theory, what May is espoused to doing away with. For May – and for her chief of staff Nick Timothy – economic activity should be moral: put simply, an international company should not be able to wreck a community while paying no tax (something, incidentally, which Jeremy Corbyn would agree with). In her first – and, as it turned out, only – speech in her campaign against Andrea Leadsom for the leadership, she also aired her wish for workers to sit on company boards. These instincts – which no doubt derive from the influence of her political hero Joseph Chamberlain – have so far not managed to prosper within the crucial realm of reality. For instance, on the issue of the proposed nuclear power station Hinkley Point, May could do little more than let it be known that she was displeased with the idea of China owning a significant stake in our nuclear power industry: after a period of mild protest, she let the Osborne-era plans go ahead. This pattern repeated itself when it came to the £23.4 billion takeover of ARM – the UK's sole world-leading hi-tech electronic company – by SoftBank, the third largest public company in Japan. This takeover was a deal which might have been designed to annoy May: ARM employed 3,000 people, and was of particular importance to Cambridge, where it has its headquarters. But here again May and Philip Hammond fell in line with neoliberal orthodoxy, stating that the sale had turned a 'great British company into a global phenomenon'[9]. It could have easily been a statement from the Osborne Treasury.

Would a May government, ratified with a big majority by the 2017 electorate, feel more confident when faced with these sorts of problems? Very possibly – but as usual with May, we do not know.

On education, we arguably have a little more to go on: the subject of her maiden speech to the House of Commons in 1997, it is the policy area she most naturally gravitates towards. The key text is May's somewhat grandiosely entitled speech to the British Academy, 'The Great Meritocracy'. In this, in addition to arguing for more grammar schools – the part of the speech which rather predictably, but to her apparent surprise, grabbed most of the headlines – May made some interesting proposals. She suggested an amendment to future access agreements,

9 R. Peston, Facebook post, 18th July 2016.

whereby universities would be required to sponsor schools in return for higher tuition fees. This policy dates to the Blair administration: the idea was originally put forward by Lord Adonis – the Minister for Schools from 2005-2008 – and was best articulated in his 2012 book *Education, Education, Education*. Adonis' work draws attention to the importance of an active state within the academies programme. Adonis is an advocate of retaining the right to use central and local government in order to improve failing schools, or close failed ones. Would the liberal-conservative side of May have the same will to make the system work that Adonis, with his belief in a busier state, plainly had?

In the same speech, May also argued that faith-based Catholic schools are more effective than faith schools set up by other groups – Muslim, Hindu, Sikh and Jew. The prime minister appeared to be recalling her own education as she explained how:

> [Catholic schools are] more ethnically diverse than other faith schools, more likely to be located in deprived communities, more likely to be rated Good or Outstanding by Ofsted, and there is growing demand for them.[10]

Finally, May stated that she wishes to see private schools do more to earn their charitable tax breaks – such as set up state-sponsored schools and also fund

10 G. Eaton, 'Theresa May's education revolution means more than just new grammar schools', published in *The New Statesman*, 9th September 2016.

places to more children from poorer backgrounds. George Eaton, writing in the *New Statesman* was among those impressed: 'With a majority of just 12, and the epic task of delivering Brexit, the Prime Minister may yet find that she has overreached. But May has shown that she is not content merely to hold power – but to use it.' Expect ideas like these to be fast-tracked if she wins a big majority.

Promising as some of that might seem, on health and climate change – the areas of government she came to the leadership knowing the least about – May has not necessarily distinguished herself. In both instances, alarm bells began ringing at the time of her first reshuffle – the deregulation-happy Andrea Leadsom has never seemed a suitable cabinet member, and especially not at Environment, where sensible regulations are most urgently needed. In the same breath, May also missed the opportunity to remove the much-disliked Jeremy Hunt from his position as Secretary of State for Health. In that area, May also scrapped the £800 million NHS bursary which was intended to help midwives and other health professionals complete their demanding training – and it is still not clear quite how that policy is mean to help the JAMs who cannot afford private healthcare and overwhelmingly need a thriving NHS. May also watered down Cameron measures to tackle obesity, which would have introduced restrictions on the sale and marketing of unhealthy foods: under May, only a small tax on sugary drinks would go ahead. Again, since the problem overwhelmingly affects working class families this was another decision that seems to rather contradict her stated intention of levelling the playing field: the small state Conservative triumphed over the One Nation Conservative. On climate change, May has at least continued with Britain's involvement in the Paris Agreement, but this is not an area where her priorities lie, and there remain fears that to secure her free trade deals, she will indulge in an 'environmental race to the bottom'. As with health, these are serious omissions and it would be naïve to rely upon her to do better a second time round.

Nor does May particularly strike one as a natural on foreign policy – a weakness pointed out by Kenneth Clarke at the outset of her premiership. During her time in parliament, May has cast interventionist votes in respect of military action in Iraq, Libya and Syria. There is no particular reason to think she will change tack should she be granted a large majority. One possible reason why Donald Trump, prior to the March 2017 strikes in Syria, didn't inform May about them sooner is that he thought she wouldn't be interested. Indeed, we can see that in the case of Scotland, May is mainly concerned with not permitting the break-up of the United Kingdom: to do so would give her more foreign policy. But prime ministers can't avoid the wider world for long – her Falklands and her Iraq may well be lying in wait. All that can be said is that we have no reliable guide as to how well she'd handle a foreign policy crisis – but then, to some extent that is always the case with prime ministers.

SO AGAIN: WHY?

In Doris Kearns Goodwin's marvellous history *Team of Rivals: the Political Genius of Abraham Lincoln*, the writer is at pains to stress the importance of timing in politics. Had Lincoln sought to emancipate the slaves sooner, he would have fallen foul of those who were fighting predominantly to preserve the Union. Had he waited too long, the war would have lacked the vital meaning it now has – the sense that all that killing was not for nothing. I do not wish to compare Theresa May to Abraham Lincoln: she has none of his folksy charm or poetic force. But still one is forced to admire the way in which she has proceeded step by step through her in-tray thus far. There is something consummate about her: even if one disapproves of her policies, one can see that this is a person with an intimate sense of power. Calling this election has, at the time of writing, the feel of a killer blow delivered at the right time *for her*. If, as seems possible, she has not secured a satisfactory agreement with the European member states by the time the deadline set in motion by the triggering of Article 50 expires in 2019, then she has given herself three years to recover before facing the electorate: had she not called this election she would have been far likelier to face the electorate without a deal in place.

Other considerations may have played their part. It has been reported that around 30 people, including a 'raft' (perhaps 20) of Conservative MPs are currently under investigation by the Crown Prosecution Service on charges of having exceeded their expenses in the 2015 general election. By calling the election, May has outmanoeuvred the CPS since any charges would have had to have been made beforehand. 20 resignations from 20 Tory MPs would have been a majority-busting affair for her. We are not in a position to be sure of the truth of this: but this, together with the perceived weakness of Jeremy Corbyn, adds to the sense that this was an election called not in the national interest, as the prime minister protests, but in her own. Indeed, it may even be diametrically *opposed* to the national interest: it certainly wastes valuable time which might have been spent in getting on with the EU negotiations. It is possible for May to retort that she is aiming for a 'stronger hand' but this argument feels bogus: one would prefer her to state that she is making a naked grasp for power than to insist that her every waking hour is spent deciphering what is best for a country, 48 per cent of which she seems to find woefully misguided in their core beliefs.

But in any case, unless the Liberal Democrats can win enough MPs to force a coalition without May at its head, all this must ultimately cede to the gigantic complexity of Brexit. It may be that this election will come to seem a small fact next to what May has already done in interpreting the Brexit vote so stringently, and in setting the wheels in motion for Britain's divorce from Europe.

In this sense she is lucky that her chief adversary, who in other respects could hardly be more different to her – a man whose ideals precede his policies and not the other way round – has been as difficult to read on Brexit as she has.

Christopher Jackson is a London-based writer. His books of poetry include The Gallery *(Salzburg, 2013) and* The Monkey Fragment *(Originals Plus, 2017). His non-fiction books are* The Fragile Democracy *(Eyewear, 2016) and* Roger Federer: Portrait of the Artist as a Sportsman *(Eyewear, 2017). A book on Theresa May is also forthcoming from Eyewear.*

LABOUR: THE ONLY WAY IS UP

by W Stephen Gilbert

The gift of prophecy is not A Thing. Very many people have deluded themselves into believing that it is, though, especially those who 'know' what the result of the 2017 general election will be. Some of those who 'know' are in the Labour Party. Luke Akehurst, among the bitterest critics of Jeremy Corbyn, described Labour's general election campaign as 'charging into the valley of death'; just what you need to keep your spirits up.

This is despite the extensive evidence that the opinion poll findings, lucratively sold to newspaper proprietors who like to offer results that square with their editorial line, are in fact worthless. Hence we have everywhere 'Labour can't win' – from the people who brought you 'people won't vote to leave the EU', not to mention 'Trump won't be president'.

Of course you, gentle reader, have some considerable advantage over me, harassed writer. You're reading these words much nearer the electoral endgame than I wrote them. In between times, there will have been a slew of local election results and those, being actual votes on actual ballot papers cast by actual voters, will have been a more authentic pointer than any opinion poll. Even so, these local results will have been an unusually poor indicator of what is to come in the national result, for it was unprecedented that local elections should occur *during* a general election campaign, and inevitably these local elections were driven almost completely off the media's agenda. Only the dedicated news channels carried live news – there was no results service on any of the leading non-specialist television channels and BBC2 alone offered a couple of post-mortem reports. So if the local turnout turned out to have been around 20% or even less, the very unrepresentative nature of the size of the poll will have distorted the result. Not so much to go on after all.

Make no mistake, though: the big story of this election is the certainty among almost the entire politico-media establishment that the result is a foregone conclusion. It's big because that consensus creates a dynamic of its own. It offers a self-fulfilling prophecy. It determines the nature of the mood in which people go to the polls and activists apply themselves to get them there; and just imagine the psychological impact on the candidates. At the same time, it defies the electorate to confound its assumptions, to announce that the people may not be bought for the proverbial mess of pottage. In that way too, it casts Jeremy Corbyn as unmistakably the underdog, the outsider or – allowing him to riff on the possibilities – the man of the people against the machine, the antithesis of 'politics as usual'. It also risks for Theresa May that a feeling of revulsion may creep into the electorate against what might be perceived as a sense of entitlement, as taking the people for granted.

But the Tory propaganda machine and its

media supporters have carefully prepared a catch-22 for Labour. Those who decline to accept the 'inevitable' are 'in denial'. This phrase from analysis has escaped into the general conversation as a useful closer of arguments, a QED. The only available counter to one's assailant who uses the locution 'you're in denial' – 'no I'm not' – is of course the very one that the assailant hopes for. If, on the other hand, the Labour supporter tries to address the possibility of defeat, such an attempt is roundly mocked as 'preparing your excuses in advance'. The clinching rebuttal to this pincer movement is for Labour to win the election. At least the satisfaction inherent in that outcome – in which case we shall be trotting out Gore Vidal's remark: 'the four most beautiful words in our common language: I told you so' – provides urgent motivation.

Much else will have taken place during the days between the writing and the reading. 'A week is a long time in politics,' Harold Wilson famously declared and, equally celebrated, Harold Macmillan remarked that what changed politics was 'events, dear boy, events'. In the interim, there will certainly have been events: rows, gaffes, jokes, surprises, retreats, developments, lies, announcements, extraneous happenings, perhaps even scandals. All these will have shaped the drama and there will be more to come. An election campaign is long enough for many things to shift, even for resignations and replacements. And anyway, Trump and Kim Jong-un could have seen us all off before June 8th.

One thing that *usually* happens in the course of election campaigns — I stress usually because we have seen this century that politics is much less stable, reliable and regular than it used to be — is that the opposition is apt to gain support. This is because opposition parties get more media coverage during election campaigns than at any other time, and there is much truth in the old saw that all publicity is good publicity. Many people do vote purely on recognition of a candidate's name. You may think your own vote is significant and influential, but it is offset by thousands that are piffling and generated by nothing remotely indicative. Democracy gives just as much power to the *shlemiel* as to the scholar.

Another thing that usually happens is that trends and movements in the electorate's sympathy gather pace just before — and even during the course of — election day. This is another reason to discount opinion polls, the data of which (even where it has not been massaged — 'weighted' as the pollsters call it, to give the process a spurious patina of scientific suggestion) is always obsolete by the time it is published.

So will Labour's 'poll rating' be much closer to that of the Tories by the time you read this, and further by election day? The correct answer is: no one knows. The opening days of the campaign made it abundantly clear that Sir Lynton Crosby, the manipulator-in-chief of the Tory propaganda machine, had determined that May v Corbyn was the winning notion on which to fight the election, and this has translated into the chanting of the mantra 'strong and stable government' by every spokesperson every hour on the hour, whether or not it is appropriate. Hilariously, Theresa May was asked in a Radio Derby interview what her view was of the term 'mugwump', applied by Boris Johnson to Jeremy Corbyn, and her knee-jerk response was to bang on again about strong and stable government, demonstrating that, whereas she likes to have carefully scripted 'jokes' to hand with which to put down Corbyn at PMQs, she doesn't actually command any wit and has no light-on-the-feet resources with which to manufacture any.

This strategy challenges Labour to undermine it. That's not so very difficult. I sent Andrew Gwynne (the MP charged with running Labour's campaign) a slogan suggestion: 'It's Not About Her – It's About You' and he was gracious enough to reply with a thumbs-up emoji. Labour certainly can make headway if it changes the narrative to one of policy and of need rather than one of demeanour and of bluster. The Tories seem short of policy proposals that are not already familiar and several of those pursued under May's leadership have had to be abandoned.

The other mantra chanted remorselessly by Tory spokespeople – it has even been uttered by Tim Farron of the Liberal Democrats – is 'a coalition of chaos'. It's difficult to understand why this might be thought pertinent or penetrating now. Analysis of voting in the 2015 election seems to confirm that there was some traction then for the Tories in suggesting mendaciously that Labour would try to make a coalition with the Scottish Nationalists or even UKIP. Lynton Crosby understood that the five years of coalition since 2010 had been unpopular, so he raised the spectre of more of the same with a different cast, meanwhile skilfully elbowing the punishment for the past coalition onto the Lib Dems in 2015's so-called decapitation strategy, targeting the seats of that party's leading MPs.

But no one will buy the notion of an anti-Tory alliance now. Corbyn nipped it in the bud decisively and promptly. One benefit of the lack of televised debates has been that there is no image in the electorate's eye of disparate opposition parties on the same platform and especially of that profoundly resonant image of Plaid Cymru's Leanne Wood, the Greens' Natalie Bennett and the SNP's Nicola Sturgeon warmly hugging each other while Ed Miliband wanly looked on at the side of the stage. Indeed, the electoral understanding that does seem to have developed is one between the Tories and UKIP in seats where the sitting Tory was identified with the Leave campaign. Labour might usefully make something of that: a coalition of closed-mindedness, perhaps.

Undermining UKIP is an important task in this campaign. UKIP support is strongest in Wales and the English north-east which, significantly, are the two areas least affected by immigration. Labour should highlight this and assure the electorate that it will never be the UKIP-lite party.

Then there is the possibility that the decapitation strategy will be reversed on June 8th. Given that both Labour and the Tories have bridged the divisions in their respective parties by asserting that, whatever else happens, the democratic will of the people (voting to leave the EU in the referendum) is sacrosanct, the Lib Dems find a certain amount of electoral territory yielded to them in their unabashed support for the EU, perhaps even to the extent of revoking or rerunning the referendum. Given the pain (little of it seemingly located in anything tangible) that is evidently still felt among those who voted to remain, there are electoral opportunities to be taken (*viz* the Richmond by-election). This ought to damage the Tories more (on the theory that the Lib Dems will aim to recover lost ground) but there might be casualties for Labour, especially in London where EU support remains strong and where Labour has been seen as the status quo in inner boroughs and in those areas that combine squeezed city dwellers and more comfortable but perhaps more frustrated commuters. That London now has a Labour mayor who is as fervently pro-EU as he is fervently anti-Corbyn may cost Sadiq Khan's party dear in the London results.

Nevertheless, winning from a position of hopelessness is something Corbyn has comfortably pulled off before. When he scraped enough MPs' nominations to squeeze onto the party leadership ballot paper in the spring of 2015, bookmakers (a more realistic guide than opinion polls) reckoned his odds at 66/1. Yet in a four-way contest, he won the leadership with more than half as many again as the combined total votes of his challengers and fully twenty per cent more of the total vote than anticipated by the last opinion poll to be taken before the ballot itself. It was the most emphatic leadership endorsement in British electoral history. Even so, Labour MPs, ever oblivious to the danger of self-harming, obliged him to seek re-election as leader, a contest in which he merely further increased his dominance, despite the party machine working long and hard to exclude from the right to vote thousands of identifiable Corbyn supporters.

The discrepancy between the reading by opinion polls of the strength of support for Corbyn and the support revealed in voting (at least up until the EU referendum) ought to give every forecaster pause, not least Theresa May. As I have written, I am no believer in surveys, but others are, and a recent poll of Labour Party members suggested that, despite all the faeces flung at him over more than eighteen months, a majority of the members would vote Corbyn leader at a theoretical third asking.

As a potential successor, John McDonnell (who has said he would not stand) was preferred by 30 per cent. McDonnell's nearest rival and the most popular social democrat was Chuka Umunna at 16 per cent. Umunna dropped out early in the 2015 leadership contest. If this poll is wrong, it is wrong big-time.

In the same survey, members were asked about their level of trust in certain institutions and people. The results were striking:

The media: trust 9%, distrust 90%
Opinion polls: 19%, 80%
The BBC: 29%, 70%
The PLP: 44%, 52%
The Shadow Cabinet: 72%, 26%
Corbyn: 98%, 2%

A health warning: the election had not been called when this survey was taken and different circumstances do produce different results. Even so, it's telling that distrust in the media is almost as great as trust in Corbyn. In October 2016, the Media Reform Coalition commissioned a survey into public attitudes to various policies. This found majority support for anti-austerity measures, an increase in public spending, tax rises for the wealthy, public ownership of the railways and removal of private sector involvement in the NHS – all policies espoused by Corbyn – yet it also found a perplexing majority belief that the Tories would be more likely than Labour to implement these policies, even though they are palpably (including in their own words) less likely.

The chair of the MRC, Justin Schlosberg, said: 'We feel that much of the media have been more preoccupied with dismissing Jeremy Corbyn as 'unelectable' than with seriously reporting on the policies he represents ... This is not about a failure of communication on the part of Labour so much as a failure of nerve on the part of a great swathe of the news media. Without a change of approach, our democracy is in deep crisis' (reported by the *Huffington Post*, October 13th 2016). I would call it a conscious bias rather than a failure of nerve. But Corbyn's team needs to highlight encouraging data. It isn't rocket science.

There is much comfort to be taken in these findings. An election campaign is the best possible opportunity for an opposition to get coverage for its policies, even if it is only via the scorn poured on those policies by rival parties. Provided Labour can see off the perennial Tory charge that the party is spendthrift and 'anti-business' for ideological reasons (rather than redistributive for practical reasons), its identification with popular proposals should get through to at least some of the electorate.

Something else will have happened between my writing these words and their emergence blinking between soft covers. The parties will have published their manifestos. At the time of writing, the commentator can only guess; Labour's National Policy Forum Consultation was still ongoing and the views of party members were still being sought. Whether these views would impact on decisions already taken is moot; your guess is as good as mine. Like any diligent party member, I put in my pitches. Democracy is a wonderful thing, but it has to be arbitrated. Labour supporters must trust that Corbyn and McDonnell, Emily Thornberry and Diane Abbott will arbitrate boldly and sensitively. I do, but then what's the alternative?

Before the manifesto launch, Labour was already committed to giving all workers, whatever their status, equal rights immediately; raising the minimum wage to £10 per hour (which bests the Tories' best target for 2020 by £1.25), including abolishing the lower rate for under-25s; building a million new homes in five years; re-introducing rent controls; abolishing zero-hours contracts and un-paid internships; banning the undercutting of Brit-ish workers by the employment of cheaper foreign labour; scrapping the public sector pay cap; repeal-ing the Tories' Trade Union Act, rolling out sec-toral collective bargaining and maintaining workers' rights despite no longer being answerable to Brus-sels; ridding the NHS of outsourcing and integrat-ing it with social care and mental health services; re-versing the increase in class sizes that have consigned 40,000 primary school pupils to classes of 36 plus and 16,600 of above 40; providing universal free school meals (interestingly, only attacked by the Tories on cost grounds, not ideologically); punishing big busi-nesses that use their size to take advantage of small suppliers (a policy particularly that can claim thou-sands of enthusiasts); transforming the increasingly squeezed public transport network by driving out private profit; tackling discrimination against wom-en in all its forms; bringing digital technology into line with Labour's egalitarian instincts; reversing the cuts that have reduced arts and library services support; doubling paid paternity leave; introducing saints' day bank holidays. Watch out for the Tory argument that 'this can only be achieved with a strong economy'; it means that they're surrendering the ideological argument to Labour.

Labour have promised that all their undertakings will be costed in the manifesto. It has been a peculiarity of politics for over a century that the Tories are 'trusted' with the public accounts in a way that Labour is not. So Labour always has an economic mountain to climb and it's a mountain that Tories can readily and easily refer to, expecting to benefit from the reference.

In fact, Labour governments have been more successful at reducing the public deficit than Tory governments, but you cannot expect the Tory-supporting media to reveal that. Until the global economic crisis of 2008-9, the deficit under Labour was negligible. But since the coalition took over in 2010, the deficit has been higher than it was in the aftermath of the crash, and only returned to crash levels (let alone pre-crash levels) in 2015. Neither George Osborne (in his six years as Chancellor) nor Philip Hammond since June 2016 has managed to bring the deficit back to the levels under Gordon Brown and Alastair Darling. In the fiscal year 2016-17, the UK's provisional net debt was £1.7 trillion. In 2007-8 it was £527 billion.

Average earnings will be an issue in this election – and if not, they should be. With Tory policies, Resolution Foundation (the non-partisan, living standards think tank, who know of what they speak) reckon that average earnings will take at least another five years to return to their level before the global financial crisis, and may well decline further because of austerity policies. By its calculation, the average British employee has lost £11,920 since the global crash, compared with expectation based on the economy's growth under Labour. Austerity hasn't worked, unless you're a high earner whose income has been protected by George Osborne and Philip Hammond, both of whom have a good deal of personal experience of high earning.

Moreover, Labour Party research revealed that the effect of austerity policies has continued to fall disproportionately on women, and within that finding a particular disproportion on women who are disabled and/or from a black or minority ethnic background. After the 2016 autumn statement, Sarah Champion, Shadow Secretary of State for Women and Equalities, told the Commons that 'individuals in the poorest households lose most from tax and benefit changes … low income black and Asian women will lose around twice as much money as low income white men … disabled men are losing nine times as much as non-disabled men'. The cynicism with which the Tories make the weakest and those least likely to get out to vote pay for the incentives that the rich apparently need to go to work is breathtaking.

Meanwhile, 24 Tory MPs are still being investigated for potential criminal offences over 2015 election expenses. If the police want the Tories' savage cuts to the policing bill reversed and their wages increased as public sector pay capping is abolished, they should take a page out of the playbook of the FBI director James Comey and make an eleventh-hour announcement of further investigations. That could be a game-changer.

Doubtless as you read these words with election day still in the future, opinion polls will still be supplying commentators with the raw material on which to build their confident anticipations of the result. Unreliable on everything, opinion polls are peculiarly poor at detecting abstract notions like determination, provocation and hope. There are, after all:

REASONS TO BE CHEERFUL

1. Opinion polls are not votes in ballot boxes and they are rarely a trustworthy indication of actual voting intentions; often they are out by miles. Remember Heath in 1970, Major in 1992, Bush in both 2000 and 2004, Cameron in 2015, Leave in 2016 (even YouGov's exit poll on the night exactly reversed the real result), Trump in 2016. I do see that all those results are less liberal than the opinion polls predicted, but the Dutch election this spring indicated an electorate more left than the polls and the French election has revealed a retreat from the established parties, evidence of which the polls only detected very late. Voters are getting less tribal, more volatile.

2. Oppositions get much more exposure during elections than they usually do, so if they have a good case they can expect to grow support. This happens with election campaigns.

3. The BBC will be coming under increasing pressure to be much more scrupulous about balance during the rest of the campaign than they have been so far, and indeed ever since Corbyn's election as leader. But if they continue presenting the main narrative as how more or less overwhelming the Tory victory is going to be, we must all inundate them with complaints. It's not too late.

4. Labour clearly has the policies that people want. The Tories only have the EU negotiations to talk about because they anticipate (but won't admit to) a decline in public finances and cannot commit to new spending, while the policies we know about (grammar schools, anyone?) aren't helping them. It shouldn't be difficult for Labour to shift the electorate's interest onto bread and butter issues. There may be some who will vote according to some mad notion that they can still keep Britain in Europe, but I don't somehow think they're numerous enough to return a Lib Dem administration.

5. Corbyn is on his third major campaign in three years, front and centre. He's at his best when campaigning, firing up audiences and drawing energy from them. Let's also remember that May has never led a campaign (she made one speech during the EU referendum; Corbyn made 123) and has poor platform presence.

6. The activists including the superbly organised Momentum have also had plenty of practice in the last two years. The war on the ground and in the social media is there to be won.

7. May was in a bind about debating on television. She looks confident with baying backbenchers at her back, cheering her every disobliging thrust at Corbyn, but she knew she couldn't get away with that in a set-piece television debate. She'd be on a hiding to nothing. Better to take the flack for ducking it; still, it's a mark against her. Corbyn is good at debates, but he has also declined to debate the other parties; without May, there'd be little advantage for him. May has confined herself to tightly controlled soundbites, surrounded by acolytes, which will have grated on some viewers. And enough voters to be significant are seeing that Corbyn happily submits himself to the public as well as the media.

8. The BBC will go on finding vox pops to say that Corbyn is 'an idiot', which seems to be the term of choice. There will still be people who feel that way on June 8th, but there will be significant numbers who, having paid attention to him for the first time, will say: 'oh, he didn't seem an idiot after all'.

9. Up until the referendum, Labour did better in every by-election than the polls predicted. That's a further reminder about the unreliability of opinion polls.

10. If the registration campaign produced a surge, especially among the young; if the ac-

tivists keep up their canvassing and can mobilise massive forces on June 8th; if members of the PLP who criticise the leadership are being sufficiently rewarded with complaining emails and tweets; if Corbyn has been given a chance to present himself to the electorate as he is rather than as the Tories and their media backers present him; then a brilliant, heart-stopping victory is absolutely possible.

W Stephen Gilbert is a writer, journalist and television producer, specialising in drama, politics and the arts. His writing has appeared in all the serious British press and in dozens of magazines and periodicals. He is the author of five books including Jeremy Corbyn – Accidental Hero, *published in 2015 by Eyewear Publishing.*

LOVE AND POLITICS: THE LIBERAL DEMOCRATS

by Russell Hargrave

This chapter is about working for, and voting for, the Liberal Democrats. It is also about the Brexit fallout, the strange world of Jeremy Corbyn, the contradictions of Theresa May, and immigration policy. But I could have called it A Short Article About Love.

Not because I love the adversarial bits of politics. While some political geeks may live for ideological arguments in pubs or angry protest meetings, I do not. But with all my heart I love politics at its most human. Discuss the state of the world with a taxi driver and I get a buzz just from exchanging views; find a new political interlocutor on Twitter and I am happy as a spring lamb. Politics at its best is a social force, leading us to try and understand one another, to disagree and try and work out our differences. It can come easily or it can be messy, but it is the most uplifting way for people to work through their passions and frustrations together. Politics is about relationships, and I adore it.

And the Liberal Democrats? Like all good love affairs, I can date when it started. In 2007 I was working as a constituency caseworker for a Lib Dem MP. This meant meeting with local people, normally several dozen each week, and going through whatever problem confronted them, to see if the MP could help. A typical set of files on my desk would include applications for better social housing, complaints about bin bags ruining the street, some parking disputes and various attempts to work out constituents' immigration status (a much more complex issue than I had ever imagined). There were more quixotic tasks thrown my way by anxious local folk, too, memorably including the need to calm down a young mum who was worried about stretch marks. Simon Hughes, the Lib Dem MP in Southwark for thirty-two years, was right when he wrote in the *Guardian* in 2010: 'Democracy is good and effective when people know who their MP is, feel they can approach them, know what they might be able to do, and are guaranteed a top-quality personal response as far as possible all year round'. The issue on my desk that morning a decade ago was an unusual one. A British-Iraqi man, a surgeon at a local hospital, was very nervous about travelling to the US. He had relatives there, whom he was desperate to see. But we were three years into the second Iraq war and his Iraqi mates had told him (rather unhelpfully) that his background might lead him to be hassled or even detained. He had turned up at the MP's advice surgery. What could she do? About the extraordinarily slim chance that US border guards would detain him? Nothing. But about his nervousness? As it turned out, we could do plenty. I phoned the surgeon and we had a chat. He was a lovely guy. He asked if he could pop into the office. I said OK. It became clear quite quickly – not that he put it this way – that the

Iraq war had shaken him. He needed reassurance that a bloody conflict between the land of his birth and his new home would not diminish the respect in which he was held in the UK. He had contacted the MP because he needed to know that a parliamentarian had his back. A visit to her advice surgery, a telephone chat with me and then a long conversation in her small HQ convinced him that she did. The surgeon didn't need anything else. He left reassured, even happy. His trip to the US was a success.

The MP was elected to look after 70,000 constituents, and some days it felt like half of them were emailing or beating a path to our door. Yet not once did she suggest I spend less time trying to find the right words for this single individual, as he struggled with his standing as a UK citizen. He had not come to his local Lib Dem MP because he wanted a letter of support or for us to harangue officials on his behalf. He wanted someone who would listen to him and, using the authority of the office, settle his nerves. The MP wanted that for him, too, and I was given all the time I needed to make it happen. That is what the Lib Dems mean to me. Support. Reassurance. A sense of place, of community. And, yes, love.

I hardly invented the idea that love and politics are linked, of course. The echo of Norman Kirk, who served as a Labour Prime Minister of New Zealand in the seventies, is deliberate. Kirk is justly remembered for an observation which remains one of the truest statements in politics: citizens in pursuit of meaningful and fruitful lives need 'someone to love, somewhere to live, somewhere to work and something to hope for'. More than forty years later, we might be tempted to recoil from something which seems a little *too* neatly-packaged, a little too good-natured for our more cynical age. We might even sniff something a bit saccharine in the air, and decide we are too sophisticated for that stuff now. But if we recoil then we are badly under-estimating the public. Politics has changed since the seventies – remade by dramatic changes to industry and demographics and communications – but the basic values on which people build their lives have shifted remarkably little.

It may seem like politics is constantly set in angry mode these days (and the 2016 EU campaign was pursued in an especially terrible temper on all sides), but there is no sign of Kirk's values diminishing. We still need to talk about love. Here, for example, is Marc Stears, whose New Economics Foundation think tank has polled thousands of people since the referendum to try and understand what drove voters on both sides and what they expect to happen next. Certainly, Stears argues, you initially hear unpleasant things from some Brexiteers about welfare claimants and interfering bureaucrats, but

> keep listening, and you will hear something else. You will hear people yearning to gain some purchase on the places where they live, and the forces which shape their lives. You will hear people desperately seeking some way of taking control

over the things that matter to them – their work, their homes and the prospects for the people they love.

There they are again. Love. Families. Hope for the future. All of which tells us something else, something which the Lib Dems will need to be careful about but can still capitalise on. Brexiteers disagreed with us about the EU in last June's referendum, but that does not make them *wrong*. The general election is a chance to invest again in our relationship with these voters. Their values are not some great mystery to us. They share the same broad sense of society and community and the party can, and should, be talking their language.

Some political activists like to pretend their side has a monopoly on looking after society and making good economic policy. This is patently silly, especially if you back a small party. As a friend once suggested to me, it is pointless being a tribal Lib Dem, because there aren't enough of you to make anything happen on your own. She had a point.

Nonetheless, we enter the election as the only main party offering a vision of the country which is both realistic and optimistic. We have the right instincts about the best way to help people 'gain some purchase on the places where they live', as Stears puts it.

The Lib Dems will have a good election. They understand how values work in politics; they understand that a party needs a suitable narrative to transmit those values to voters; and they understand how to grind out that narrative so that people remember them in the polling booth.

Working to establish a clear message is not a very sexy bit of the political armoury, it's true. The dark arts of opposition research and rapid rebuttal are much more compelling than the long-game of planning and sustaining a story for the party to tell. But the truth is that the Lib Dems responded to Brexit much more swiftly than their rivals. We were a party in search of a distinct identity – a third party in a system dominated by two parties is pretty much sunk without one – and suddenly a cause landed in our lap.

And not just any cause. As a political subject, Brexit is the dominant game in town. There is some disagreement among pollsters about how dominant it is, whether it swamps absolutely everything else or merely looms over every other topic like a gravestone, but there is little doubt that people have defined themselves by their decision in the EU referendum. It has transformed the political landscape. People decided that they were either Remainers or Brexiteers, and they expected political parties to pick a side too. Which gave the Lib Dems, electorally on their knees just months before, a plumb target. 48 per cent of the British public had voted to stay in the EU, and plenty more voted to leave without any commitment to Brexit at its most reckless. It is a decent audience for an instinctively pro-European, internationalist, centrist party to design a narrative for.

And so we did. The Tories made their pitch to the right (promising a hard divorce from the EU, opting for the twin economic risks of ending free movement and exiting the single market). Labour vacillated haplessly between the two positions (as late as April Shadow Foreign Secretary Emily Thornberry told voters that her party 'hadn't chosen a side' over Brexit).

Tim Farron, meanwhile, offered-up a simple, clear direction. The Lib Dems didn't back Article 50 because doing so gave the PM carte blanche to negotiate what Farron called 'any shoddy old deal'. He also demanded a second referendum to take place after the Brexit negotiations, so that the public could decide whether or not the government had reached a good settlement for the country. The party won't countenance the idea that EU nationals currently making their lives here should be left in the dark about their right to be in the country. These calls are morally decent and politically right. My Polish neighbours and their daughter could be deported because the government won't guarantee their right to stay in the country. My brother's job is under threat because potential foreign investors in UK science will have to work on newly unfavourable terms. My parents-in-law are worried about their life savings because they are held in more than one country.

If these values are threaded through our campaign – other activists and voters will no doubt have their own versions – there is a substantial audience who are worried, like me, that a hard Brexit threatens their security and the happiness of the people they care about. The Lib Dems have an audience out there.

Get into arguments about the procedural bits of Lib Dem policy, on the other hand – when would a second referendum be held? How would it bind the government? – and it will suck life away from the campaign. The risk hard Brexit poses is profound, but technical chat about bills and legislation is dull. It isn't relevant to people's lives. It isn't about the things voters value, and it isn't about the things people love.

I have already confessed that my party doesn't have all the best ideas, nor an exclusive claim on decency. Jeremy Corbyn's Labour has the right instincts about immigration, for example: blaming hard-working newcomers for exploitation in the jobs market is socially divisive and economically illiterate. Theresa May ushered through gay marriage legislation while at the Home Office, aided by her junior minister, Lib Dem Lynne Featherstone. Corbyn and May should be applauded.

Even if I can convince you that love is at the heart of politics, then, why do my lot deserve that vote rather than Labour or the Conservatives?

Corbyn's Labour already has its own political tradition for thinking about communities and social good. These ideals are typically now packaged under the concept 'solidarity', a cry that lay dormant on the mainstream left for years and has enjoyed a renaissance through Corbyn's backers in Momentum. The word has always had sharp edges, sharper than I am comfortable with. It conjures up images of solidarity being mustered always *against* something, set up always in opposition (to some variation on the nastiness of capitalists mainly). I am too cheerful about trade and profit, and the rights of citizens to pursue both, to reach for that vocabulary. I don't stand with my comrades against my enemies, hoping that the one will bring about the collapse of the other. When I hear 'solidarity', I don't imagine people gathered together behind a single social cause but quite the opposite: a jaundiced, brittle version of society, which needs a fight or at least a row to find meaning. This comes through in Corbyn's background, too. His long-standing passion for the rights of Latin America is mainly a vehicle for beating up America (he has gone remarkably quiet these days on Cuban human rights and the devastating poverty in socialist Venezuela). His sympathy for the underdog in the UK has led him to champion the IRA; in Middle Eastern politics it has made him, infamously, a 'friend' of the anti-Semitic murderers of Hamas. He is a cliché come alive: his enemy's enemy is his friend, no matter how wretched they may be. Healthy relationships must include a reckoning with your partners: what is the common cause which brings you together, and what else separates the values you hold dear? Corbyn's solidarity spiel makes little room for that. His political partnerships are created around a common adversary. They sacrifice civility for ideology (this distinction may help explain why Labour have been slow to deal with accusations of anti-Jewish prejudice in the party. The Lib Dems acted much more swiftly to oust David Ward from their list of potential MPs over his anti-Semitic remarks).

What about the PM? Theresa May is caught, I suspect, between her instincts and brutal political calculation. I worked on refugee policy for years, and the trafficking of human beings is a heinous crime, one of the world's great evils. It is clear that at the Home Office May had a deeply-felt passion for fighting this modern version of slavery. May can't get a grip on it, though, and this is largely her own fault. Wherever she turns to try and tackle trafficking, she will find progress sabotaged by other political calculations. The reputation May won at the Home Office resulted from hard-headed policy-making and excellent spin. For years, search May's name online and you found the phrase 'safe pair of hands'. Tough initiatives got her the headlines she needed to survive in the job. Sometimes ministers need to be strong. The public demand to see immigration rules enforced and enforced strictly, for example, meant May had an irresistible mandate to try and do that. But her stated intention of making the UK a 'hostile environment' for illegal migrants was a terrible, jarring moment in her tenure. The phrasing is just too violent, the intent too cruel. It makes the state an instrument of aggression, asking police, landlords and medical professionals to check the status of the people coming to them for help. It ought not to be necessary to point out that legislating for a genuine issue can't be allowed to blur into demonising a whole class of people. In May's case, it is. This has a serious impact on, among other issues, trafficking. Victims are very often stripped of their passports by their abusers and cut off from the communities where they live. This is precisely the grey zone where people most need the state to help, yet where 'hostile environment' policies are targeted. May has trapped the very people she wants to help. Communities can't work like this. Big policy agendas like the Shared Society, which rely on local networks and relationships, may well flounder. People are turned on one another. Hostile environments hurt all of us, and hurt the communities we call home.

The last time the Lib Dems planned for a General Election, it was as the junior partners in a coalition. We need little reminder of the outcome. The Tories sailed off with a majority government and we were given a kicking by voters (340 Lib Dem candidates – three hundred and forty! – lost their deposits). A popular refrain inside the party around this time was that *history will treat us kindly*. The history argument went a bit like this: although voters had handed the party a thrashing, we could take reassurance from the fact that eventually political experts would recognise the essential work we had done in government. That sounded like rubbish to me then and it still does now. Even then, before Brexit and the public rejection of experts, I believed that voters were the only ones who mattered. If you couldn't get a hearing from them, the fellow citizens who schlep off to the polling station every few years, then the cause was a hopeless one. All those constituents with their split bin bags and their search for new social housing – they have to hear what a party offers and find there a reason to turn out and vote. Someone else can spend time analysing the long historical view. As this new election looms over the horizon, only one verdict matters, and that will be delivered at the polling stations. I think these stories about hope and the future, wrapped up in a warning against hard Brexit, can secure votes. If it doesn't, it is a waste of time.

I will stick to my guns. The Lib Dems have spent the last twelve months doing what good political parties do: threading together policies into a sensible narrative, broadcasting their values in ways people can understand, and picking up local seats at a decent click. The whole thing is fronted by a perfectly normal politician and supported by a cast of bright young things behind the scenes.

The comparisons to Trudeau in Canada are overdone, but this can be a change election for the Lib Dems. As our election leaflets suggest, citizens have some big choices to make about the direction of the country. There is a very attractive liberal offer out there, and plenty of voters ready to snap it up.

'What's the government policy on love?' wrote the former political advisor John McTernan. 'Ask that question and you'll be laughed at'. Yet McTernan floats the idea because he knows, as I do, that the country already has policies on love. Tons of them. It is possible that some of the most arcane political business doesn't touch on our strongest values, but most will. Homes and schools. How the state helps look after our parents and how the businesses we build allow us to plan our futures. What we love and where we live, how we work and what we hope for.

No one gets it completely right or wrong, or there would be no need for politics. There would probably be no need for elections. Instead, the coming weeks promise more of the good stuff of politics: claims and counter-claims, media storms, arguments between friends and rivals.

And I already know where my heart lies. I will be voting for the Liberal Democrats on June 8th.

Russell Hargrave has worked on press and communications in the charity sector for the last seven years. Prior to this Russ worked for his local Liberal Democrat MP, and more recently sat on the committee debating party immigration policy.

THE GREEN PARTY: ASK THE QUESTIONS YOURSELF

by Rosanna Hildyard

The Green Party is arguably irrelevant in the UK general election. This is an election in which it is undeniable that the main subject is Brexit: will we or won't we, and the Green Party holds little sway. What matters in this election is getting bums on seats in parliament: a straightforward majority for either hard or soft breakfast-biscuit. The pro-Remain Greens have a small proportion of the UK vote, one MP, and only three MEPs (in contrast, *twenty* Europhobic UKIP members stood for the chance to sit in Brussels). The Green Party is relatively poor and lacks support. And yet, where the subject is Brexit, Green issues are perhaps the most important of all.

In rural areas such as Cornwall, which voted overwhelmingly in favour of Brexit, EU policies often mean a great deal in daily life. For farmers, Brexit will mean an end to continental restrictions on farming practices – the use of chemicals, the treatment of animals and so on. The promised reassessment of strict continental regulations could give farmers more of a chance to beat the unpredictable British weather in their constant battle against and alongside the natural world. Speaking at the Oxford Farming Conference in January this year, the President of the Country Land and Business Association, Ross

Murray, insisted: '[The UK] can achieve increased productivity and improved environmental outcomes though a new world-leading food, farming and environmental policy.'

But can it? Having the same regulations from Spain to Settle, East Anglia to Transylvania is surely nonsensical. Landscapes and farming practices are different. The UK's primary producers deserve specific attention. But cutting Brussels' red tape could be dangerous, and is at the very least short-sighted. For example, one of the EU's most significant areas of power is over the use of chemicals in production. If released from Brussels' blanket limitation, UK farmers could be able to use far stronger pesticides on crops, leading to increased production but a downswing for biodiversity – a very real impact for the UK's richly varied wildlife and habitats.

We are already seeing this in effect, with Andrea Leadsom's announcement that one new piece of regulation will be to scrap the 'three-crop rule', a system of rotation which enforces some degree of biodiversity in larger farms. Without this law, large farms will be able to relentlessly till the land with the same crop year on year, creating monocultures out of what was once a delicately balanced ecosystem. Even Glastonbury gets a fallow year to recover from chemical misuse.

Craig Bennett, head of Friends of the Earth, calls Brexit a 'red alert'. Brexit will mean weaker safeguards to the environment in all areas. The Tories have already shown themselves to be dismissive of these concerns in a stampede for free trade capitalism, a divided Labour is focused on immigration, employment rights and the single market, and the Lib Dem angle is entirely about reversing to Remain. It is the Greens, alone among UK parties, who prioritise environmental policies, and yet it is not just immigration and the economy that will affect us in Brexit, Green issues are among the most important changes we will face.

Already we can see that the UK's wildlife and environment will be affected by Brexit, and that Green politics are a necessary consideration in the Great Debate of In or Out. Yet the Green Party's own efforts will be largely fruitless. It is no good considering the Greens as a political party that might have clout at Westminster by themselves. What they do have, however, is influence.

It is true that two Green MPs across the UK do have a chance of being voted in in the general election. Electing Molly Scott Cato as MP for Bristol West, and the Green Party a second MP, is the party's 'top priority' for GE 2017. In 2015, 26.8% of the vote in Bristol went to the Greens, against 35.7% Labour. Similarly, Caroline Lucas, the Green Party's only current MP, is likely to retain her seat in Brighton, with a 41% share of the vote in 2015 – a strong lead against Labour's 27.3%. However, in both university cities, the Greens' main rivals are Labour. There are no constituencies in which the

Greens directly threaten the Tories. If you're interested in voting tactically for a soft Brexit, you might as well vote Labour.

In this election, the outcome depends on our own tactical voting and the politicking of major parties. Depending on your constituency, voting for Labour even if you'd prefer a Lib Dem might be the best decision, if you're hoping for a government that's favourable to the EU. Similarly, if the parties work together to put the country first, Lib Dems, Greens and UKIP might reduce their individual totals, but put together a majority for a softer, or harder, Brexit – and perhaps more favour from one of the larger two parties during the new government. And, at time of writing, the first definite signs of tactical politics have come from the Greens. On the 21st April 2017, the Green Party members of Ealing Central and Acton, where they had previously won 1841 votes, voted not to elect a candidate, in order to allow the Labour candidate hopes of a strong majority. Rupa Huq, now a Labour MP, gained a majority of only 274 in 2015. In 2017, she has promised to keep a Green agenda, to campaign against a third runway at Heathrow, and for voting reform and the environment – key areas of the Green manifesto. At this point in the election, it is the Green Party who are pushing the progressive alliance agenda in UK politics – and in return, their demands are being taken seriously by the other parties.

Another area where the Greens hold strong cultural influence is in their leadership. The Lib Dems are notorious for broken promises and collaboration in the Tory-run coalition. The race for the Tory leadership revealed vicious infighting between the power-hungry in that party, and Labour continues to collapse in on itself, with the majority of sitting MPs openly contemptuous of Jeremy Corbyn. Perhaps because of the lingering hangover from the expenses scandal, professional politicians seem to be held in lower regard than ever. Yet the leader of the Green party, Caroline Lucas, is largely trusted. A YouGov poll taken by academics at Queen Mary University of London this year revealed the levels of trust held in major politicians and party leaders. Lucas is the politician most trusted by Londoners, though the prime minister and Sadiq Khan also have high approval ratings. Jeremy Corbyn and UKIP leader Paul Nuttall trail far behind.

On the 23rd April 2017, Lucas topped the Environmental Funders' Network's list of 'environmental heroes', ahead of the universally adored David Attenborough – could she be our next national treasure? Lucas and her co-leader, Jonathan Bartley, are given a great deal of airtime and media coverage. Even though the high regard she is held in may not directly translate to votes, her presence in UK politics is not small. Though the Greens currently hold only one MP, Lucas' determination and personal appeal stand the party in good stead. There is the risk that if Lucas goes, so does Green credibility. Indeed, the Greens suffered when Lucas stood down as leader in favour of Sheffield candidate Natalie Bennett – a far less charismatic actor on the political stage (and unknown in comparison to Lucas' celebrity). Lucas is a sensible, likeable and humorous woman of great integrity, who has done much to drag the party away from an image of placard-waving hippies and tree-huggers without diluting the Green radical message, and gives credibility to politicians such as Bennett and Bartley. Certainly while she is leader, and for this election, the Greens matter.

And Lucas, the Green's first MP, was only voted into Parliament in 2010. The Greens are relatively young in the national sphere of political influence, and they may be the party of tomorrow. Once we have voted, for either hard or soft Brexit, the new government will be focused on deciding the path the UK takes for the next 50 years. And there are signs that the Green Party will be powerful in the near future.

Though Greens do not currently promise to figure greatly in the results of the General Election 2017, the size of the party has grown exponentially in the 21st century. In 2001, membership of the Green Party stood at 5268 members; in 2013, 13,809; in 2014, 30,900; in 2015, 63,219.

Political scientist Sarah Birch noted 'Green voters have tended to be younger and better educated than the electorate at large, and they are known to be more likely than most voters to work in the public sector'. She also points out the strong correlation between areas of high Green support and areas with a high percentage of those who define themselves as having no religion. Although the Green Party themselves claim their members 'come from all walks of life', they have a disproportionately high volume of support from young, university-educated people, in university cities. These voters – young, engaged, likely to vote – are important electorally. These are the cultural consumers to whom the media wants to appeal, and in fact the creators of media themselves. Building loyalty among young voters will stand the Greens in good stead for the next decades.

The Greens also have influence at a grassroots level. Since the early 1990s until 2009, the number of Green Party local councillors has risen from zero to over 100. Local policies and neighbourhood volunteers are hugely important to the Greens. A key part of Jonathan Bartley's successful bid for co-leadership was local activism in his home, Lambeth. Fighting library closures and high-street pollution is not exactly what one imagines disturbing the sleep of the politically pragmatic Theresa May, or idealistic Corbyn.

This, of course, has both pros and cons. The Green Party is a truly democratic party in terms of its policies, and is anti-big government. Unlike the Tories, Labour, and Liberal Democrats, policy is developed from the ideas of ordinary members, which are voted on at a conference. The party places an especially high value on co-operative collective politics. And leaders like Bartley – ordinary people, voluntary activists – might spark genuine emotional responses in voters. The Greens might be criticised for lack of professional experience. Some voters think only professional politicians can make a success of government. The Greens are still marginalised as out-of-touch, idealistic radicals – but the fact that Green activists are often devoted volunteers is not necessarily a criticism. The party is well-organised and credible. What they lack is the financial backing (from unions and corporations) that the larger parties have. The Greens do not have the money to spend on big ad campaigns and therefore cannot compete. At the moment.

If you're considering voting for the Greens or supporting their policies in the election, these are the things you need to know:

Obviously, the Greens stand for environmental protection. They ask us to prioritise climate change as a threat to life, and are committed to investing in renewable energy and reducing reliance on fossil fuels. They aim to transition to a zero-carbon economy, banning fracking, phasing out coal power and refusing new nuclear power stations.

In 2015, they promised to make sure that everyone in the UK lives within five minutes' walk of a green open space. They would create land and marine conservation zones and impose strict limits on development and traffic around woodland areas and National Parks. They would ban cages for hens and rabbits, and also the production and sale of foie gras (surely something the Tories would never do), as well as enhanced education around treatment of animals. Perhaps in a few decades, the treatment of animals in large farms and laboratories is something that will disgust us. We must consider whether animals and wildlife are something to distance ourselves from. Can we ignore these issues any longer?

But the Green Party no longer appeals solely to those taken in by the climate change 'hoax', as Donald Trump calls it ('the concept of global warming was created by and for the Chinese in order to make US manufacturing non-competitive'), and those who dislike the idea of force-fed-goose liver. In the last election, the Green Party's manifesto begins with a chapter on the economy.

The Greens are agitating for a Universal Basic Income, a non-means-tested income which would cover all basic needs, to replace benefits and tax-free allowances. They would impose maximum pay ratios in companies, so that a CEO could not earn more than ten times the amount of its lowest-paid employee. They also believe investment in renewable energy and other green technologies could be the basis of an innovative, healthy economy.

Overall, the Greens support the NHS and public services, including investment in public transport and free university education. In April 2017, Jonathan Bartley criticised Trident (the Greens would scrap Trident and all the UK's nuclear weapons). Speaking at St George's Hospital in Tooting, Bartley said: 'With people struggling to get by in Britain, it's inexcusable to be ploughing people's money into this cold war relic.' Instead, he said, the Green Party would use the multi-millions spent on Trident in order to give the NHS a 'kiss of life' of an extra £3 billion every year.

The Greens, unsurprisingly, support proportional representation, which would give smaller parties more chance of election. As opposed to first past the post, an electoral system which works best for a two-party state, proportional representation of votes represents a multi-party system. However, with Labour and Tories still dominating, we must ask: is the UK really there yet?

The Greens appeal and are appealing to young people. Free university, pledges for better mental healthcare, a living wage and affordable housing. Their policies are perhaps naïve – they have not been tested in large government. And yet, when considering the Greens as a part of UK politics in 2017 political power, we should not be thinking of Westminster-style governance. We should be thinking larger: nationally, and long-term. The Green Party is asking for a different way of thinking about running the country: one with far more individual involvement and passionate ideals. This would not work for everybody, now. But the tide may turn, if we allow it.

Rosanna Hildyard is from rural North Yorkshire and studied English at Oxford University. Her fiction and journalism have recently appeared in The Isis Magazine, The Northern Echo, York Evening Press *and the political anthologies* Adrift *and* Outside Of Me, *on topics ranging from cosmetic surgery to speciesism.*

UKIP AND POST-TRUTH BRITAIN

by Oliver Jones

Why vote UKIP? You don't need to – they've already won.

Every modern European democracy has its radical, populist, right-wing edge. In the UK, this is UKIP. The UK Independence Party was founded in 1991, pledging to force the United Kingdom out of Europe. They remained on the fringe, an aside in real politics, until the remarkable leadership of Nigel Farage carved a space for them on the political map. They experienced drastically expanded influence during the successful Brexit campaign, and have just as rapidly disappeared, with UKIP poll numbers dipping to just 4% this April – less than half of what they took at the last election.

And yet UKIP's media coverage remains disproportionately large relative to their popularity and actual political power. UKIP has only ever had one seat in the Houses of Parliament, and even then only thanks to Douglas Carswell's defection from the Conservative Party and successful re-election as a UKIP candidate. Their media appearances, on the other hand, have roughly equalled those of the Liberal Democrats since 2015 – and their media mentions far surpass them[11]. By comparison, the Green Party with its single, long-standing seat in Parliament,

---

11 Nigel Farage's 25 appearances on Question Time place him 11th in all-time appearance rankings. UKIP were second only to Labour in 2015's social media mentions, with roughly thrice as many mentions as the Lib Dems and five times as many as the Greens.

gets little to no coverage. Green Party spokespeople rarely make it onto national news or chat shows[12].

Why is this? Part of the reason is what we might call the Trump effect. UKIP's uniquely British brand of ignorance, inflammatory language, barely disguised racism and anti-expert rhetoric makes for much more entertaining television than the Green Party's sober commitment to sustainability or Corbyn's stolid socialism. Another part may be simple principle. The media should represent all sides of a debate and prevent the majority voice from drowning out the independents. This would be convincing if UKIP weren't allotted such a major slice of the media pie, far more than any independent or party of similar size, and if news networks and papers weren't so obviously susceptible to frenzies of scandal and mass outrage.

A bigger part still may be a sign of the times. In the wake of the global phenomenon of post-truth, nationalist parties have already swept away established ideologies in the United States, Poland and Russia, and could do the same in France. Ethno-centric, anti-immigrant, fringe right wing parties the world over have been able to radically boost their political platform through the medium of Trumped-up, incendiary claims which turn out to be either distortions of fact or complete falsehoods.

Examples of post-truth employed by UKIP – mainly during the Brexit campaign – include

---

12 Most people don't know, for instance, that the Green Party leadership is currently co-chaired by Caroline Lucas and Jonathan Bartley. But who doesn't know who Nigel Farage is?

claims that membership of the EU costs £350 million a week (it's more like £160 million), that the EU costs us millions in 'red tape' (the benefits usually outweigh the costs) and that within the EU, the UK consistently 'loses' (we are rarely outvoted). This new attitude towards fact was infamously summed up in the Michael Gove quote 'I think people have had enough of experts'. More recently, we have UKIP leader Paul Nuttall's false claim that he lost close friends at the 1989 Hillsborough disaster – and that he is formerly a professional football player. Long before the election we had Nigel Farage claiming that Rowan Williams wanted to introduce Sharia law in certain cities.

Inflammatory right wing rhetoric is nothing new. What is new is the means by which it is distributed and the scale of that distribution. The increased traction of the bare-faced lie has a lot to do with the increasing reliance of pretty much everyone on news links generated by social media. These are ranked on the basis of number of shares, rather than on balance or good reporting. The most popular stories will be the most viral, but rarely the most true. Related is a cultivation of disregard for mainstream media by radical parties. Where fake right-wing news is lauded as a kind of grassroots information network, the 'liberal'[13] media is accused, sometimes rightly, of unfairly presenting

13 In the case of UKIP, it has historically attracted scorn from both left-leaning and Conservative-owned papers. Tellingly, outlets like the *Guardian* tend to criticise them for their xenophobic language, while Murdoch outlets like the *Sunday Times* focus on the personal failings of UKIP party members.

a right-wing party's representatives and message.

Parties who promote brash slogans and explosive news stories might be said to be 'seizing the memes of production': taking control of the culture's talking space to make their agenda the country's nexus of debate. Since almost all adults in the UK have Facebook accounts, and most of us get almost all our news stories through Facebook, our culture's talking space pretty much *is* Facebook. Dialogue which takes place in other spaces – the House of Commons, the BBC interview room, the Labour Party Conference – passes through social media before it gets to us. A party that is able to set the agenda on social media is able to profoundly affect political discussion for the whole country.

This is bad for many reasons, regardless of your party alignment. The UK is home to around 63 million people, all with their own unique permutations of economic and social anxiety. Regional concerns and the concerns of particular industries would ideally be addressed by political parties in a general election. Instead, debate tends to centre around a few core issues, with the bulk of every party's manifesto promises and PR offerings forced to centre around those issues. It's a self-reinforcing cycle, with voters hammered by the same few emotive points – immigration, membership of the EU, inequality – until politics becomes synonymous with those debates[14].

14 The exception to this is the NHS. Health came second only to Brexit in a recent list of voter issues, but receives almost no media attention in between elections, probably because health reform stories don't translate so well onto media platforms. For the most part we're limited to variations of the same headline: 'NHS in crisis'.

Clearly, some of those issues are genuinely important, but the way they completely dominate the political agenda is to the detriment of other areas of concern. It may also be part of why it is common to feel that elections have few points of contact with real life, which, unless you are a major financier, politician or global operative, is almost exclusively local.

The centralisation of debate also has the effect of creating a political deadlock on precisely the issues that are most debated. Once the entire country is gripped by partisan argument, the endless forcing of an issue by parties on opposing sides of it makes consensus all but impossible. Each side has too much to lose by conceding.

The compression of our political and social space on a single platform also means that the divisions that apply to parties apply to their supporters as well. The political differences between people are reflected in what they see in their Facebook newsfeed. Left-leaning liberals see news stories and data with a left-leaning angle – between 1995 and 2011, EU immigrants contributed £8.8 billion more than they gained. Anti-immigration nationalists see the opposite – 900 Syrians arrested in a crackdown on human trafficking (and not that there's been a massive surge in anti-Muslim hate crime since 2015).

The effect of fake news in this geared-up context is calamitous. A fake news story will spread through a Facebook 'echo chamber', acquiring increasing social proof with each share (particularly when a story is shared by a public figure). Fake news has the advantage over real news of being potentially far more shareable and provocative, limited only by the imagination of its creator[15]. Which is more likely to be shared – a wordy thesis by a political pundit concluding that there are two sides to any argument, or a screaming headline about an imminent terrorist threat?

Given the power of these kinds of claims, you may wonder why UKIP hasn't been able to do a Trump and dominate the news cycle and poll results. Relative to the Trump team, UKIP suffers from a disastrous lack of organisational talent and daring. Trump had his own now-mythically memetic pronouncements, as well as a slick campaign strategist in his son-in-law Jared Kushner, who set up trading floor-style ad generators to create perfectly pitched ads and used machine learning to target wavering voters through Facebook. By comparison, UKIP, having all but lost Nigel Farage (who departed post-Brexit in pursuit of his new, global celebrity) has fallen back on rote, uninspired fist shaking, predictably attacking Islam and immigration ad nauseam. Their message is too close to what you'd expect from a fringe, nationalist party. It quickly stopped being newsworthy and was unable to effectively seize the news cycle, or maintain the momentum gathered by Farage's highly effective Brexit campaign.

15 Some real examples from the US election: 'Pope Francis Shocks World, Endorses Donald Trump for President, Releases Statement' (that got 100,000 shares), 'FBI Agent Suspected In Hillary Email Leaks Found Dead in Apparent Murder -Suicide' (500,000 shares).

Instead, UKIP has increasingly buried itself in an anti-Islam rabbit-hole, when all gains from such a position have already been used up. Lacking the creativity and flexibility to stir real outrage, they are increasingly becoming a cliché – a peripheral party with a lot of hate but little ambition.

In UKIP's case, Brexit may have been the kiss of death. Without a clear objective to guide them, or a clear enemy once Labour and the Conservative Party accepted Brexit, UKIP was left adrift. Their anti-Muslim rhetoric stirs up hatred, but does not earn them any further support. Their policy platform is suffocated – with the Conservatives championing a hard Brexit and Labour appealing to anti-establishment sentiment. Ironically, UKIP's strongest theatre was the European Parliament, where it has twenty MEPs, making it the joint largest UK party. Brexit means the loss of those seats and the political platform that came with them.

UKIP seems to have accepted its diminished role. It is reportedly considering not even fielding candidates in constituencies where a pro-Brexit, Conservative MP is running. UKIP has been referred to as a 'gateway drug' for defecting Labour voters: the 2015 election saw many former Labour voters turn towards UKIP and recent polls suggest that those voters may now be going all the way over to the mainstream right, particularly in Wales. This would be cogent with UKIP's history. The party started, after all, as a single-issue, Eurosceptic organisation in the 90s (then called the Anti-Federalist League) whose goal was to persuade the Conservative Party to leave the European Union.

Most recently, a number of prominent UKIP members have resigned from the party in response to the increasingly Islam-obsessed policy platform. Former donor Arron Banks withdrew his support, accusing UKIP of 'going to war on Muslim religion' as the party pledged to ban burkas in public and impose mandatory medicals for Muslim schoolgirls suspected of having had their genitals mutilated by family members. Douglas Carswell, UKIP's sole MP, left the party to run as an independent. Even party leader Paul Nuttall has shown doubt as to whether he would stand for election to his own party on June 8th.

UKIP may be seen as irrelevant, after the recent by-election results of 5th May, when it gained one seat and lost 114. It is not an entirely spent force yet, however. Though it currently has no MPs, it has Assembly Members in the Welsh Assembly, and retains councilors in local government. Paul Nuttall's pledge upon being elected leader was to take votes from Labour, and, judging by the current polls, this they will do, if only by swinging them over to the Tories.

UKIP's function in the 2017 election is to feed its 2015 votes to the Conservative Party, while preying on the working-class Labour vote through its anti-immigrant, pro-blue-collar rhetoric and anti-establishment message. Post-Brexit UKIP serves, effectively, as the radical vanguard of the right, preaching the Anglo-centrism, religious hatred, imperial nostalgia and racial bitterness that would be unacceptable in Conservative Party officials. It leverages anti-Islam and anti-immigration sentiments and discharges them harmlessly as UKIP votes – ones that can no longer prop up a real political alternative. In the relationship between the Conservative Party and UKIP we see an Anglicised model of the Trump-GOP alliance in the United States, an uneasy truce between nationalism and corporate interest.

Historically, this makes sense. UKIP emerged as an expression of Euroscepticism and combined with a broader movement of right-wing populist parties. Relative to its European counterparts, the voting system in the UK favours larger, more established parties, which is part of the reason UKIP never gained much official traction. Theresa May's increasingly authoritarian administration has adopted many of UKIP's more popular positions – the Conservative Party website indicates intention to restrict immigrant access to work and housing, healthcare, driving licenses and bank accounts and introduce a 'British values' citizenship test[16]. The Conservative Party have been able to win away UKIP's electoral base while condemning the party publicly, leaving it with only its most fringe el-

---

16 The Conservative Party rather provocatively gives welfare and immigration the same webpage – claiming that 'benefits are out of control'. By combining the issues, rage against 'benefits' becomes a coded way to rage against immigrants. But illegal immigrants claim a negligible amount of government benefit, thousands of times less than the administrative cost of pinpointing those marginal cases – there's no defensible reason for combining the two issues on the same page.

ements to work with. Theresa May, meanwhile, is experiencing record levels of approval. At 62%, her peak popularity has surpassed that of either Blair or Thatcher, just months into her premiership.

So why vote UKIP? Sometimes it's cool to be bad. There's something conceptually chic about creative lies and their application. Maybe it's nice to be part of a movement. Maybe hatred of a demonised enemy creates the kind of social cohesion that could be the basis of a proto-fascistic British utopia. Maybe you enjoy seeing crazed, offensive statements in bold print. If the above statements apply to you, then Theresa May's predicted landslide shouldn't worry you too much. Why vote UKIP? You don't need to – they've already won.

Oliver Jones is a British-Peruvian writer and editor based in London. He holds a BA honours degree in Politics & International Relations from Oxford University and has edited two political poetry anthologies, #refugeeswelcome *and* #NousSommesParis. *He is author of the psychobiography* Donald Trump: The Rhetoric, *out with Eyewear Publishing.*

THE
ISSUES

SECONDARY EDUCATION AND THE GENERAL ELECTION

by Phil Brown

In an election year, education presents us with a paradox: those with the largest stake in the argument are amongst the only citizens who are not allowed to vote. The choices we make on their behalf in the polling booths will radically shape their generation through the educational experiences the country provides.

For thirty years, Britain's schools have cycled between famine and feast with each new administration – though anyone who has experience of working in schools under both styles of government will attest to the fact that the differences are just as financial as they are ideological.

I began my teaching career in 2009 as a comprehensive school English teacher in South London. New Labour were breathing their last gasps under Gordon Brown and, waiting in the wings, were Cameron and Gove ready to fundamentally change the architecture of our state school system. In the time since, I have served as a second-in-command and run a department, worked as a school social chair and a teacher-governor.

In this overview, I shall attempt to use my experience in a range of state secondary schools, with some wider reading, to elucidate what the 2017

General Election means for state education. I am of course limited by the fact that, at time of writing, neither party has produced a manifesto. Seeing as the three major parties (there were once three major parties) produced manifestos in 2015 festooned with images of politicians who now reside in back benches or non-parliamentary careers, it is arguable how helpful any such documents are in predicting the future of our country.

I also feel obliged to declare my relative ignorance of what is at stake in primary education and higher education – if my argument remains rooted in the state secondary school, it is because this is the world that, as an English teacher and the son of an English teacher, I have known my whole life.

Readers may find themselves irked by my bipartite presentation of educational issues in terms of Conservative vs Labour – I can only apologise for lacking the imagination to fully envision a curriculum under a Green, UKIP or SNP majority and the professional scrutiny to have noticed what aspects of my professional life during the 2010-2015 period were to be attributed to the Liberal Democrats. Similarly, I have not taken the measure of speculating on what various combinations of coalition would bring – such decisions are of course to be made in smoke-filled rooms and announced in rose gardens, and not to be guessed at by the likes of me.

THE STORY SO FAR

In 1996, a young politician named Anthony Charles Lynton Blair made a speech in Blackpool, outlining his ambitions for a Labour-led government. The one section of this speech which endures in the collective memories of teachers is this rhetorical flourish:

> Ask me my three main priorities for government and I tell you: education, education and education.

This was the beginning of a time of optimism and upheaval in British education. Initiatives, reforms and, most importantly, money were pumped wantonly into our schools in a way which is difficult to imagine in the pass-the-hat, austerity measures our schools are now facing. Twelve years on from Blair's mission statement, in the run-up to the 2010 elections, state schools were a shining example of the best and the worst results of overfunding. Excellent facilities and the latest technology were to be found in freshly built classrooms across the country. Excellent student/teacher ratios were provided and many excellent practitioners were tempted into the profession by 'golden hello' bursaries and a wide variety of new and innovative or non-academic and money-wasting (depending on who you ask) qualifications were offered to young people. Schools received vast sums of money for achieving 'specialist status' in particular academic fields and were able to employ hitherto unheard-of numbers of 'support staff' who could be deployed in classrooms to support the learning of those with SEN (Special Educational Needs).

But this was no utopia. The American-style management culture which personified Blair's premiership was emulated throughout the education system. The sudden proliferation of 'Assistant Headteachers' throughout the land and the creation of multifarious responsibility posts (called TLR's or Teaching and Learning Responsibilities) was a direct response to the sheer number of new initiatives which needed rolling out and the loosening of the public sector's purse strings. The result? Everyone soon became a 'Middle Leader' of one sort or another, in the hopes of one day making it into the hallowed echelons of the Senior Leadership Team. Everyone was in charge of something, and accountable to five other responsibility holders for something else. And anyone who had no interest in playing the Middle Leader game soon had to bashfully explain how they were happy to stay being 'Just A Teacher'.

Then came the Tories. Of course they had the Lib-Dems in tow the first time around, but it was hard to notice any sort of tempering of Tory ideology in these years because we had Michael Gove; the most robust, uncompromising and revolutionary Secretary of State for Education since Kenneth Baker had the temerity to introduce a National Curriculum in 1988. For many of us teaching during this era, Gove became the most unpalatable four-letter word one could use in the staffroom. Withdrawing Labour educational policies with swift efficiency, but using the existing managerial structures to its advantage, the Conservative Party has radically transformed the school system over the course of seven years. The movement to make all schools transform into 'academies' (for the uninitiated, I shall be explaining what these are later on) as well as the financial squeeze caused by reallocation of public funding means that many state schools are running on a deficit budget, headteachers are asking parents to set up direct debits to help cover shortfalls, record numbers of teachers are leaving the profession and redundancies are being made at all levels, in a sector which once drew people in due to its relative security.

SO WHAT ARE THE KEY ISSUES?

In pure financial terms, the choice between major parties is a very simple one. The Labour party will spend more money per pupil on education than the Conservatives – any obfuscation of this is numerical sleight of hand. The battle is, of course, never as simple as that and is to be fought on the following key points; grammar schools, comprehensive schools, academies and educational ideology. I shall attempt to address each in turn, in terms of how each party can be expected to behave if they are given the keys to the car.

Grammar Schools
I feel some small affinity for Theresa May, in that her and I both received a grammar school, as well as, a comprehensive school education. I have also worked

in both types of school, and consider the morality of their existence to be one of the most fruitful debates in modern politics. The Cameron / Gove administration proved to be dark days for Britain's grammar schools, at least from a financial perspective. The recalibration of funding models away from Subject Specialist Status and towards 'Pupil Premium' students (i.e. schools now receive more funding based on the number of severely disadvantaged students on their roster) means that many grammar schools (which the most recent data suggests have a relatively privileged intake[17]) have spent the past five years seeking increasingly inventive ways to make ends meet.

In an arguably calculated break from their predecessors, Theresa May and Justine Greening made clear their renewed support for the selective school system and stated their intention to build new grammar schools across the country. May has pledged to ring-fence funding to create a new generation of selective schools and free schools in a bid to tackle what she refers to as 'selection by income'.

Corbyn, an ex-grammar school boy himself, has made clear his intentions to oppose all proposals to build new grammar schools. Corbyn, writing in the *Daily Mirror* last year, proclaimed: 'Grammar schools depress overall educational achievement and siphon off a few better-off children at the expense of the rest'.

---

17 http://researchbriefings.files.parliament.uk/documents/SN01398/SN01398.pdf

So, in this sense, a stance on grammar schools is perhaps the clearest cut educational decision a voter can make in this election – May's Conservatives are lucidly for them, Corbyn's Labour are staunchly against them. Arriving at a decision on this issue is arguably the easiest way to start reaching a choice on who to vote for. But before you do, some questions that are worth your consideration:

— The state selective system vastly favours those who have received some form of private tuition for entrance examinations. How can this be a truly democratic system?
— If there were no explicitly selective schools then all students would be enrolled within their 'catchment area', meaning that people's postcodes would determine the nature of their education. How can this be fair on those living in deprived areas?
— If we take our most academically able young students away into separate schools where they get taught at an advanced level, are we not placing a cap on our expectations of everyone who didn't 'make the cut' when they were eleven years old?
— If we force our most academically able young students to receive the same education as those who require the most remedial support, are we not preventing both groups of students from receiving the level of specialised support they deserve?

— How can our comprehensive schools not suffer
  as a result of siphoning off entire cohorts of
  students who are academically able from an early
  age and come from families who value the
  importance of education enough to have
  put them in for the tests?
— How can we justify a school system wherein
  the only alternatives to mainstream education
  can be found through affluence or religion?

Comprehensive Schools
Piloted in the 40s, and then rolled out in the 60s,
comprehensives are the predominant type of British
school and they are where the vast majority of our
young people are educated. To neglect our comprehensive education system is to neglect a generation.

Corbyn has been outspoken in his desire for comprehensive school reform. Policies, pledges and utopian
desires have included:

— Reduce the number of 'super-size' classes which
  see pupils 'crammed like sardines' into
  classrooms
— Free school meals for all students (to be funded
  by taxation on private education)
— Scrapping of tuition fees for higher education

Theresa May and her comprehensive-educated Minister for Education, Justine Greening, have been
comparatively quiet on their plans for mainstream

comprehensive schools, choosing to focus their attention on the rolling out of 'free schools' and new grammar schools. It is my personal intuition that, under a Conservative government, we are unlikely to see seismic reforms of the comprehensive system in the immediate future, as Gove's impressive yet dastardly legacy means mainstream education continues to be a politically toxic hot potato, and there is still a long time to go before his reformed examination system is properly embedded. May and Greening would likely not choose to significantly shift the current Conservative policies unless they had a significant counterplan for the inevitable series of industrial actions which would ensue.

What we are more likely to see under a Conservative government is a continued decline in real-term funding for schools, resulting in higher class sizes, reduced numbers of subjects available at A Level, a shortage of teachers and increasingly nefarious ways of saving money such as:

— targeting older (more expensive) members of staff with capability measures
— increased accountability measures and a 'robust' approach from line managers
— increasingly subjective use of exam results to block pay-progression
— redundancies and the threat thereof to increase productivity
— larger cohorts

Academies

Whilst they have fallen out of political discussion in recent months, the most fundamental shift in state education, both grammar and comprehensive, has been the move towards 'academisation' which occurred under Cameron's first term as PM.

The thinking behind the shift towards making schools into 'academies' was a reasonably simple one: rather than having schools tied to supposedly nasty, cumbersome, bureaucratic Local Educational Authorities (LEAs), schools could be liberated into the wonderful independent world of academisation. Rather than rely on LEAs for financial support and spending restrictions, an academy could be reborn as the architect of its own destiny, free to restructure all elements of its day to day running to suit its own unique needs. In short, 'academisation' is the educational equivalent of 'deregulation'. What could possibly go wrong?

What followed for many schools was a swift realisation that 'going it alone' as an academy was an unprecedented financial burden and very quickly burnt through the funding reserves. The answer to this problem? Become a Multi-Academy Trust, thus sharing resources, funds and risks with a number of schools and become part of a recognisable 'brand' of schools, complete with an Executive Headteacher who oversees all of the franchises alongside an Illuminati-esque faction of overseers.

Much has been written about the benefits and difficulties faced by the swathes of schools who 'academised'. Criticisms have been levelled at the existence of 'Executive Superheads' who draw large salaries from the schools they oversee whilst being largely absent from their day-to-day running. Similarly questionable is the existence of a 'Board of Trustees' for a Multi-Academy Trust which, in many ways, trumps the governing body of its constituent schools whilst having a far less representative number of members (no teachers or parents, for example). Academies also have a significantly lower level of accountability to teacher unions.

So, how do our candidates feel about this incredibly complex and, frankly, politically ungainly issue?

Corbyn himself famously clashed with David Cameron on the topic of academies in April 2016, choosing to use all of his PMQ questions to grill him on the effectiveness of these forced 'top-down changes'. Likening them to Jeremy Hunt's impositions on junior doctors, Corbyn clearly made the point that he sees academisation as a move towards removing job security and working conditions from our education workers.

Theresa May is likely to avoid discussion of academy schools, as they are a clear hallmark of the previous administration and a distraction from the stamp she wishes to make on the premiership. To defend academies is to align herself with Gove and Cameron, and to refute their value is to align herself with the opposition, so I should imagine that May will simply treat academisation as an inarguable fact of life and work from there.

It is highly unlikely however, that either party in power would seek a public discussion on the existence of academies for the plain reason that, like Brexit, a school's decision to become an academy is a bell which is nigh on impossible to unring. So for now, they are likely here to stay.

EDUCATIONAL PHILOSOPHY

Whilst each new administration has its own particular spin on educational philosophy, and each individual borough, school and subject-department has its own particular experience of the ensuing reforms, there are a few broad strokes to be drawn on the style of education our children are likely to receive depending on the party who holds power.

1. Modular Versus Linear Examination

Twelve years under Labour taught educators to fear the dreaded words 'Controlled Assessments' – the series of pseudo-exams which students would sit over the course of their GCSE education as they gradually accumulated points towards their final grade. There was much to admire about this approach – it broke courses into a series of specialised projects and spread the stress of examination periods into relatively manageable checkpoints. It also meant that students could prepare answers to specific areas of study, rather than learning a large body of knowledge for an examination which would only test a very small percentage of it.

Because Controlled Assessments shifted the

responsibility of marking, moderating and invigilating onto teachers, however, they also lead to some incredibly mendacious practices in certain schools where pressure to succeed outweighed professional integrity and all manner of methods were employed to keep the departmental spreadsheets singing a happy tune. Not to mention the increased workload of marking a whole class-set of lengthy essays every half-term on top of your existing workload.

By contrast, end-of-year examination is the favoured approach under the current Conservative government. No more coursework, no Controlled Assessments, just straight-forward terminal examinations. Gone are the days of knowing with some certainty what 40 per cent of a student's grade is before the exam season begins – it is all resting on those final tests. This is a favourable method in terms of ensuring that students have a wide, adaptable understanding of key topics and making sure they keep a working memory of them for several months after it has been covered in class.

It also means that schools have a far looser grasp on how their students are actually faring and question-setting for summer exams can drastically alter the performance of a whole cohort. It is also incredibly difficult for students who suffer from a range of Special Educational Needs to perform under exam conditions for such a sustained amount of time within a relatively short period with so much riding on their performance.

2. Skills-Based Versus Content-Based Learning

If previous policies are any indicator, then we can expect a Conservative education to continue to steer towards the ethos of assimilating vast bodies of knowledge which can be learned by rote, and judging expertise more against breadth of knowledge than shrewdness of application. From an English teacher's perspective, this approach usually lends itself to curricula full of lengthy novels, vast anthologies of poetry and a focus on 'knowing the classics'. Moreover, exams are engineered to make sure that students have indeed studied the *whole* of any given text, rather than token extracts.

By contrast, a Labour-lead curriculum tends to be more skills-oriented. Large bodies of knowledge are usually made into extract-based anthologies which give students a broad overview of topics and the emphasis is very much centred around demonstrating skills as discrete competencies. In the past, this has meant that students have not had to study entire novels and plays as long as they are able to demonstrate certain methods of analysis, such as close reading, comparison, retrieval of evidence and response to an isolated extract.

In short, Tory and Labour educational policies have traditionally favoured two different versions of intelligence – the Conservative model often being characterised as rigorous, Dickensian book learning and the Labour approach often being lampooned as watered down 'bitty' modules in which students are taught to temporarily blag their way through writing about a topic. In truth, both approaches have tremendous value and are certainly not mutually exclusive.

3. Cultural Capital versus Cosmopolitan Diversity
Needing little explanation, the issue of what subjects are taught in schools and what aspects of them are covered is at the heart of party difference. A Conservative educational system will continue to favour 'the canon', and what the Department for Education currently refers to as 'British values'. In real terms, this will manifest itself in the texts which students study, the version of history they will learn, the artists they encounter, the types of guest speakers they listen to and the types of school trips which will (or will not) be subsidised. A derisive critic of this educational paradigm might find themselves tempted to dismiss it as a series of lessons about how wonderful white men have been throughout history (apart from during Black History Week).

By contrast, Labour-led curricula have always favoured the importance of diversity. The arts, the humanities and religious studies have led the way under Labour governments in promoting a wide breadth of voices and cultural perspectives on educational growth and have arguably led to one of the most culturally accepting generations of young people in the country's history. Yet criticisms have often been levelled against the approach towards representation in Labour-lead educational initiatives which can arguably lead to tokenism and false equivalence when presenting each text, historical event or religious practice as being one side of an equally weighted argument with an evenly balanced counterpart to match it.

CONCLUSIONS

I have avoided extensive discussion of the country's potential secretaries of state for education for two reasons: firstly, Jeremy Corbyn is known for haemorrhaging shadow ministers at the speed it takes Alastair Campbell to set up a WhatsApp group, and secondly the Conservative Party has proved itself to be hardly immune to playing musical thrones in these volatile, populist times.

But a brief word on our potential candidates. In Justine Greening and Angela Rayner, we have two potential secretaries of state with much to admire. Greening embodies the ethos of social mobility that she preaches and has the academic background to intellectually face down her detractors. Those who are hoping for increased spending on the public sector may baulk slightly at her background in economics.

Another success story of social mobility, Angela Rayner's background as a teenage single parent with no qualifications and a trade union representative make her a potentially vital force for improving the lot of comprehensive students and teachers and her (at time of writing) loyalty to Corbyn is likely to give education the inside track. Given her age and educational experiences, though, voters may question her understanding of further and higher education.

Neither candidate has the visionary qualities of Michael Gove, yet neither has the same elitist, ruthless qualities that led him to make public aspersions about an entire profession and betray his oldest friends on an international platform.

So, in short…

Vote Conservative if you:
— Believe in grammar schools
— Think 'The Classics' and 'The Canon' are the keystone of education
— Favour terminal exams over modular coursework
— Want the 'academy' system to quietly stay as it is
— Are happy for state schools to rely on parental contributions for funding
— Don't mind class sizes rising a bit
— Are happy to stick out the occasional teacher strike
— Think the current teacher recruitment crisis will sort itself out when we've got rid of all the grumbly nay-sayers
— Think exams have been getting too easy for too long and students need a dose of difficulty
— Quite like the idea of replacing letter-grades for exams with the 9-1 number system

Vote Labour if you:
— Are against grammar schools
— Support free school meals for all students
— Think skills and application are more important
  than memorising information
— Think modular education is a more valid
  yardstick of ability
— Want state schools to be reclaimed from financial
  incentives
— Want more money pumped into schools
— Don't mind the occasional 'white elephant'
  policy that appears and vanishes in a flourish
  of wasted time and money
— Want potential teachers with impressive
  qualifications to be lured into the profession
  by strong salaries and good job security
— Think class sizes need to be reduced
— Are OK with the prospect of sacking off
  this bizarre 'Grades 9-1' experiment and
  returning back to the good old reliable
  A*-U configuration you're used to

Vote for a third party if you:
— Have faith that a coalition can produce a
  meaningful, coherent sense of direction to
  the future of our education system
— Believe that the enemy of your enemy is
  your friend and simply wish to keep your
  least favourite party out of power

Don't vote if you:
— Believe that if you quietly let things run their course then they will always turn out for the best

There are, of course, more issues at stake during this election than education, though few talking points are more telling as to what seeds a government is willing to sow. How will I be voting? For what it's worth, Labour. Is it because I am a *Guardian*-reading, public-sector, leftie, millennial Corbynista? Perhaps, but perhaps my conviction is borne of seven years' experience of what Conservative rule has done to our schools, our teachers and, most importantly, our students. Has it been without success? Absolutely not. Were New Labour without their vast educational shortcomings? Absolutely not. But can our current state education system survive without a vast allocation of public funding being delivered where it matters, rather than soaked up by the invisible machinery of increasingly ruthless multi-school conglomerations? Absolutely not.

Phil Brown is a writer, editor and high school English teacher. He was born in South London where he lived and worked until 2016. He now lives abroad, teaching in an international school.

THE NHS: A SPLINTERED HEART

by Adam Steiner

The 2017 snap election is the definitive event that threatens to take the NHS to breaking point. The recent years of Conservative government have seen a calculated and purposeful 'dismantling' of the National Health Service. This term has become a recurring motif in almost every newspaper and television report discussing the future of health policy in the UK.

The signs of wear and tear in the social fabric of the NHS are clear for all to see: increased waiting times, both in A & E and for life-saving operations, the failure to retain hospital and GP staff placed under increasing pressure to do more with less (work harder, for longer without a pay rise), alongside a sharp decline in the standards and quality of care. All of which has lead to an increasingly negative perception of the NHS, undermining public support for the service and its staff. As the UK population grows, lives longer and with more complicated healthcare needs, the NHS is more vital than ever. But the question remains – who is responsible for its perceived decline: is it being destroyed from the inside by government cuts, or is it an outmoded service, no longer fit for purpose? The outcome of this general election could force the greatest changes ever made to the NHS as we know it, or even its complete liquidation.

In this essay, I will explore four key issues

of issues upon which the struggle for the future of the NHS will be fought: the psychic schism over the social value focus of the NHS, the right to access care, different party proposals for safeguarding, restructuring or dismantling the NHS, and the gradual loss of care that government cuts have engendered, known as death of affect.

A WRECKING BALL TO PROGRESS

The NHS has always been a key voting issue in the UK – such is the level of public and personal investment in its services, it can sway voters to shift their allegiances and energise politicians into action, at both local and national level. It sits near the top of any serious political party's election manifesto, dominates newspaper headlines and unites voters from all walks of life. To ignore the NHS and the key questions about its financial sustainability, the service's physical capacity and the need to maintain standards is political suicide – for any party.

All of the major parties contending seats throughout the 2017 General Election have made commitments to the NHS, of varying degrees of vagueness. So far Theresa May of the Conservatives has only stated that her party will 'continue to invest' in the NHS – said without irony. By contrast, Jeremy Corbyn has so far vowed to 'reverse marketisation' and 'integrate services for the elderly and disabled people'. The Liberal Democrats have argued for a 1p increase in income tax towards NHS funding while the Green Party have pledged to decentralise healthcare management to local authorities, and to increase NHS funding – without saying how.

I would argue that the most immediate challenge the NHS presents to any political party is to accommodate, and maintain, the left-wing ideology of its creation which has continued to define its purpose, identity and structure. The initial mantra for NHS care, 'from cradle to grave', evoked the principle by which healthcare should be made accessible and universalised over each individual's lifespan. This is enshrined in three key particulars:
— That it meet the needs of everyone
— That it be free at the point of delivery
— That it be based on clinical need, not ability
to pay

Any changes to the NHS that act in direct contravention of these statements can be seen as an attack upon the healthcare system itself. The 1948 launch of the NHS holds an awkward position within what has since become known as the British Welfare State – when the 1942 Beveridge Report proposed a system of social insurance that would protect British citizens with basic income support for the sick, unemployed, elderly, families and their children, such that citizens could bounce back from hardship with the minimum of state support. Beveridge's findings achieved cross-party support and, it is commonly believed, helped secure an election win for the Labour party in 1945. But the NHS has since become tainted by many of the negative associations people now make about the modern benefits system.

The NHS is universal in so many ways, occupying a strange status akin to the mercurial analogy of church and state. It deals so intimately with the minutiae of people's lives that its remit inevitably crosses over into the realm of social care – with regional NHS Trusts and local authorities often working in partnership to help manage many complex needs.

The NHS is also a great resource of political people-power, currently employing more than 1,200,000 staff. From cleaners and porters, to nurses, paramedics and doctors, to chief consultants and trust managers, all are NHS patients, the majority of them union members; they are also taxpayers and voters. And it would seem natural to assume that many of these people would vote in accordance with the Labour party that founded the organisation. This feeling is borne-out by the current #publicduty hashtag that has seen many NHS staff take to social media, arguing that it is an ethical duty of their medical role to vote for the Labour party, and to encourage others to do so as well. The organisation remains socialist at heart.

But the solidarity within the NHS has been changing for many years since Tony Blair's Labour government of the late 90s and early 2000s moved away from recruiting more ground-level staff in favour of introducing new levels of management. This created a preoccupation with administration, monitoring processes and top-heavy internal and external evaluation.

What Conservatives might term a dense

and costly bureaucracy has arguably grown worse under their own practices, and continued to generate a divided spirit of working for the NHS. While non-frontline admin, secretarial workers, statisticians and managers are a necessary part of the NHS, their role remains focussed around recording, monitoring and analysing targets; this function is more or less exclusive from direct provision of care. This kind of work attracts a certain kind of employee, less invested, more likely to move on and seek new career opportunities in the business sector, or to aim for internal promotion. Their hearts are in it, but not in the same way as a nurse's or a doctor's is. They are also less likely to be unionised and more likely to vote for another party besides Labour, more out of personal interest. So it is that the NHS has become more like a business chasing shadow efficiencies, and less like a cooperative where everyone was invested in the pursuit of providing social value through care.

THE GOOD PATIENT

The NHS is strongly connected to the workings of the UK benefits system (and the Department for Work and Pensions) by virtue of its majority funding from general taxation, with a small amount being contributed by National Insurance payments. Equally, both services directly and indirectly support disabled people, others with congenital illnesses or individuals suffering from severe mental ill-health, many of whom are too ill to work. These people are also the greatest victims of government austerity and its determined policy of deeper and deeper financial cuts to all public services and benefits, including carer allowances, long-term healthcare social work. It is these people who stand to lose the most from further changes made to the NHS.

In his book *Chavs* (2011, Verso) the journalist Owen Jones defended these same individuals as being subject to a vicious mass-media and pop-culture stereotype that turned the public against the working classes and benefit claimants, degrading them as pseudo-criminals who abused the system at the expense of taxpayers and, to use the now-ubiquitous and elitist term, 'hard-working people'.

Conservatives have always tended to steer away from what they term as nanny-state interference. But now, the extent to which someone is ill and qualifies for state-supported assistance is being questioned and set against lifestyle choices of individual responsibility. A blame culture, much like the one Jones discussed, has become rife – we are quick to judge who should access NHS services and question the basis of their need. There is a strong movement of fat-shaming; attacking the life-saving treatment of obesity, contrasted with people requesting surgery such as stomach staples for cosmetic reasons, as well as the treatment of addiction. It is hard to stand in defence of alcoholics needing liver transplants and ex-smokers suffering from lung cancer, but in keeping with the spirit of the NHS they have as much right to access services as anyone else.

Even more contentious are the largely inflated arguments that the NHS is being overrun by 'healthcare tourism'; opportunists who visit the UK with the express intention of being treated for free by the NHS. It was first noted by numerous tabloid papers amid a smear campaign in the early 2000s, when there was a sharp rise in eastern European people from newly elected EU-member states coming to the UK to study and look for work. This caused a violent and disgusting reaction in some parts of the UK; a perceived crisis of identity and the authenticity of some imagined sense of Britishness, leading to the rise of pseudo-political parties, such as the BNP and UKIP, springing up and embracing the lazy populist vote, embracing racism and fear; masquerading as freedom from invasion. The recently-published essay collection, *The Good Immigrant* (Ed. Nikesh Shukla, 2016, UnBound), which discusses British attitudes towards race, citizenship and social acceptance, responded by asking what constituted the acceptable face of immigration in UK today. This question has become one of the most divisive political issues within the Brexit campaign, and has had direct negative implications for the future of the NHS and race relations. The Brexit campaign sold the easily digestible ignorance of white van man's burden to the masses and so many voters jumped on the now-notorious big red bus that bore the slogan: 'We send the EU £350m a week, let's fund our NHS instead' – a claim which has since been shown to be false and, judging by the voting records of many pro-Brexit MPs, deliberately misleading. Many

Brexit voters might now feel cheated by British politics (because they were) so re-engaging them as voters in the general election, which *will* have severe and direct consequences for the NHS, might prove all too difficult.

The immigrant, 'good' or 'bad', was vilified to the extent that many medical staff of foreign national status within the NHS might be denied the right to remain in the UK or fail to be granted citizenship, and be forced to leave the NHS and exit the country; or even choose to leave due to fears of rising intolerance in Brexit Britain. Yet again, the UK suffers from hypocritical paralysis in which droves of British-born doctors and nurses have moved to (the former colony) Australia where wages and working conditions are significantly better than within the NHS. This double-edged fallout has created a staffing vacuum, weakening the service and providing a convenient excuse for the government to engage more external, private healthcare provision.

However, there is a problem with the picture of healthcare tourism and the number of non-taxpaying individuals using, or abusing, NHS services. The actual costs of this situation are estimated as being up to £300 million for health tourism, and visitor and migrant NHS use at £2 billion – both figures are a fraction of NHS expenditure which sits at around £100 billion per annum. Most of the £2 billion visitor and migrant expenditure is thought to be genuine, and is supplemented by fees levied in accordance with recent changes to the Immigration Act of 2015.

Clearly, all human beings, as patients, are entitled to free care at point of access, but some are more entitled than others.

CURE THE NHS / KILL THE NHS

The NHS is vast and expensive – much of the Department of Health's £110 billion budget of 2013-14 was spent on the National Health Service. Contrast this amount to the government's call for NHS trusts to combine in helping to create efficiency savings of £22 billion. Due to advances in modern medicine, people are living longer but with more complex healthcare needs as they progress into old age. Older people also draw state pensions and require long-term NHS and social care support – stretching NHS capacity in terms of both longevity and capacity. Older people also vote in considerable numbers, their intentions more commonly informed by long-standing party allegiances, as opposed to concrete policies.

It's hard to put a price on good health, along with quality of life, which is highly relative. Health is the ultimate form of social value, and to some extent, it transcends money, class and background – in that it affects everyone. Consequently, any politician standing in the 2017 General Election must be able to offer strong policies for managing the future sustainability and affordability of the NHS.

There is no clear political solution to cure the NHS of its many ills; there is more of a generic battle cry that is must be 'saved', such is the common fear from its staff that it is under threat. Equally, the Conservative government can offer no absolutist solution without proving devastatingly unpopular and extremist. In 2015 David Cameron was so keen to show his support for the NHS and win generic public approval that he borrowed the slogan 'the NHS is safe in my hands', from former PM Margaret Thatcher, who promised Britons the same thing back in 1982.

If we are to accept that the current government holds at the very least a nascent desire to 'dismantle the NHS', or at least take it down a peg or two, then it is likely that their strategy must include plans to splinter the service; in healthcare provision, public image and the solidarity of its staff. Whether through benevolent laissez faire strategies, such as opening up market restrictions for independent healthcare providers and insurance, or contracting out more NHS work – both actions result in immediately factionalising the NHS and its patients; to divide and conquer, if you will.

The extreme differences between the Labour and Conservative ideologies that must inform their approaches to the NHS will inevitably lead to the two parties taking polarised positions, deepening the rift of voter intentions. They will share a common problem; avoiding direct taxation while improving services, and the problem of appearing quite similar in this approach, but remain very different in spirit.

Labour must back the NHS to the hilt in a bid to ensure it remains true to the service's original vision that is echoed still in the party's current far-left agenda, manifested for many by the staunch and stalwart figurehead of Jeremy Corbyn, who has proposed an increase in national insurance contributions.

By contrast, the Conservative Party must find increasingly surreptitious ways to present a defensive approach towards the NHS, as a burnt-out ward requiring a strong hand. Their aim will focus upon creating new empowering 'options' for individual patients, driving forward a tiered system of external contractors working within the NHS and external private insurance-based healthcare providers, who will lure away anyone to part with cash in order to escape the queues, fear of infection, and over-worked and stressed-out staff. This generic proposal – to lessen squalor while reducing the tax dollar – would sound appealing to any voter – especially those who have the money to pay for premium healthcare services. Alongside this, there are proposals for contributory payments, such that people pay £10 towards a GP appointment, in order to encourage attendance and dissuade lateness. What would be considerably more difficult would be any kind of minimal indirect contribution payments, like a membership subscription for breakdown services, towards services that someone might never use.

This does create the potential for tiers of class-based service within the NHS – in direct opposition to the founding aim of equality in access to healthcare. The Ryanair – cattle trucks in the sky – treatment of access to NHS care has the built-in association of right-wing aspiration for the exclusivity of premium and priority services; for class divides to become entrenched in a system that was designed to treat everyone according to need. Another angle on this is the precarity of elective surgeries. These are relatively routine operations that people with a range of conditions undergo to alleviate pain or to control symptoms, often relating to a disability or chronic illness. It is foreseeable that such operations might be made less available to patients, or that they are required to contribute towards their cost, making them unaffordable for some. It is particularly shocking to imagine that money and personal connections might become the key factors that determine how and when some patients live and others die.

Equally, there is a corruptive aspect of increased privatisation for people with a duty of care, driven by results. There has been a pay freeze on all public sector staff, including NHS nurses, that is set to continue until 2019. Private companies are likely to offer better working conditions and rates of pay, leading to a direct drain on the NHS as some of the most skilled and experienced workers cross over to the other sector. It makes sense in terms of each individual choice, but when the NHS is compromised to the extent that it is forced into the position of facing 'healthy competition' we see the NHS being dragged back into the area of big business, in which it cannot, and was never designed to, compete.

Just recently NHS consultant Ian Paterson was convicted of carrying out more than 250 needless breast operations, forcing the NHS to pay out almost £10m in compensation and causing a lot of pain and suffering. His motives remain questionable, but the main argument seems to be that Paterson forged cancer test results in order to extract cash from insurance companies for his own personal profit. The key point here, is that when people's lives and wellbeing are weighed against greed, profit and pay, these are strictly incompatible motives in the maintenance of ethical standards and a duty of care.

A further point is the biased position of many MPs who vote in accordance with and actively promote the inclusion of NHS work being contracted out to private healthcare firms and their lobbyists. Around 70 MPs from across the parties are shown to be investors in, or having received donations from, a range of private healthcare providers, which thwarts any possibility of impartially safeguarding the NHS and its independence. Once again, it stands as a direct business competitor to these shareholders.

DEATH OF AFFECT

Mental health is one of the largest factors in determining the future of the NHS – it is directly tied to increased pressures upon NHS staff and austerity measures placed upon people with mental health issues.

One in four people will suffer from some form of mental ill-heath during their lifetime, and one in ten from severe or enduring mental ill-health – rates of incidence comparable to cancer figures of 1 in 3. Mental ill-health is the invisible illness, and because many conditions are long-term and can never be entirely 'cured' they are some of the most expensive for the NHS to support. They are often treated or managed through a complex system of social care support, a range of benefits and NHS therapy or medication.

As social care systems increasingly 'break down', due to social workers becoming mentally unwell due to stress, increased levels of responsibility and growing caseloads, GPs are relying upon medication alone, what was once known as the 'chemical cosh', to treat mental ill-health; the most laissez faire and ineffective approach, which for many does little on its own to improve an individual's quality of life. In a bid to reduce NHS costs, crisis services, often the first point of contact, are being stretched to cover more cases, while there is a drive for increased 'through-put' of clearing psychiatric in-patient beds, occupied at a cost of £400 per day, with pressure placed on psychiatric staff to send home high-risk patients, sometimes just 24 hours after a suicide attempt. The human cost of this is considerable, with a sharp rise of 26% in the number of suicides under some form of NHS psychiatric care (up to 751 in 2015).

This is also reflected in the mental state of over-worked NHS staff, pressurised to deliver on increasing targets, with female doctors twice as likely to commit suicide as a general member of the population. In fact, three female junior doctors from the South West of England have gone missing or committed suicide in the last year. What happens when a member of staff is too busy, too tired and under too much pressure to make the sufficient investment of care in their patients? Coupled with the exposure to frustration, anger and sometimes physical abuse from patients who feel neglected or unfairly treated, staff can become numbed, crushed between cuts from above and a sense of unfulfilled obligation toward patients – the lack of opportunity to do their job.

This scenario is comparable to what the author JG Ballard termed death of affect. It is underlined by a loss of empathy we would expect in most people, and certainly in medical staff, when forced to care under factory-process conditions. It often presents as a sociopathic mindset or even dissociative traits, where people fail to act to the utmost of their abilities, or at all, in helping others more vulnerable than themselves. At their most extreme, such behaviours breed cruelty, and resignation towards a failure to help. In this environment, the limits of individual responsibility are harder to delineate between the hands-on staff and managers, let alone the politicians who impose drastic financial cuts, increasing working hours and unrealistic targets.

This trend is directly tied to a growing toxic cycle of alienation that is being engendered between government, NHS staff and their patients. A Marxist reading of the situation might seem alarmist, but consider the growing spirit of mistrust, sense of doubt and loss of faith that is being raised on all sides against the NHS. Such is the intensity of death of affect that the regime of austerity generates a feed-back loop of unfeeling, feckless ignorance and the ultimate cost-saving scenario – death.

To examine how far the lines have been drawn between government and NHS staff, consider the junior doctors' strike on the 26th April 2016. With the support of the British Medical Association 21,608 junior doctors, almost 80% of those due to work on that day walked out of hospitals, making it the largest NHS strike in the last 40 years. The movement was a reaction against the government's imposition of a new contract that would force junior doctors into a monthly rota of 'weekend' shifts, that actually take place over Friday to Monday (four days), without any increase in pay for anti-social hours. Much like the show of force in the 2003 1 million-strong protest against British involvement in the Iraq war, a significant amount of noise was raised, and yet the contract changes were still pushed through by Health Minister Jeremy Hunt. The strike also led to around 100,000 operations being cancelled, which might have further alienated public support for their cause. Such is the pressure and scrutiny NHS staff face in their responsibilities. Even with the eviscer-ating tactics of Margaret Thatcher's closure of coal pits and the military shutdown of the miners' strike, she was not brazen enough to openly manipulate and attack the next generation of NHS workers.

VIVA LIFE!

In the most philosophical sense, I believe that the measure of a society should be the manner in which it cares for its most vulnerable members. The future of an under-funded, class-tiered and case-by-cost NHS would mean that those with what might be termed the lowest quality of life, the poorest health and the most complex needs, would be the first to suffer. Some of these people are not judged to have sufficient capacity to be able to vote – so in the eyes of some politicians, they are citizens that count for less, perhaps even less than human.

It is hard to voice the unthinkable, to imagine just how bad it can get: full-time care for extremely disabled people cut, older people being forced out of their homes and into hospital or even patients being allowed to die when they cannot afford to pay a medical bill and do not have insurance. If there is a battle for the body and soul of the NHS, then it will be settled by the 2017 general election – and its outcome will be final.

Adam Steiner has worked as an NHS cleaner and mental heath development worker. His first novel, Politics of the Asylum, *about his experiences working in the NHS is published by Urbane Publications (2017).*

TRIDENT

by Aaron Kent

I hold the distinction of having lived a rather jux-
taposed life for a few years – I was an anti-Trident
submariner. I lived among Trident II D-5 ballistic
missiles upon HMS Victorious, and slept not far
from the UK's nuclear deterrent, and the whole time
I despised both myself and the job I was doing. This
isn't to say that I hate the decent, hard-working submariners who populated the underwater behemoth
alongside me, or that I think my specialist area, sonar operation, is an undeserving or unnecessary job.
I just always felt uneasy about the nuclear deterrent,
our nation's need for it, and the dangers of nuclear
grandstanding.

First and foremost, before understanding
Trident, and making your own mind up about its
purpose[18] and the need for it, it is key to get an insight into the vehicle for these ballistic missiles, the
submarine. Therefore this essay will be split into two
sections – the first covering the submarines, the second, the Trident missiles themselves.

VANGUARD-CLASS SUBMARINES

The UK has four Vanguard-class submarines: Vanguard, Vengeance, Victorious and Valiant. Each of
these has the capability to carry Trident missiles, and

---

18 I think it is clear that I already hold a well-formed opinion on Trident, and this will probably be clear throughout. But please always try to look at both sides and inform yourself of all
the facts before making your mind up. (This is good advice for politics in general, I feel).

to act as an active deterrent at sea. The idea is to always have one V-class submarine at sea continuously, ensuring that the UK is ready to react at a moment's notice. Yet, there is another, more subtle reason for such a determined approach to patrolling the oceans – the Strategic Defence Review of July 1998[19] states there is the capacity to avoid misunderstandings by keeping a continuous at-sea deterrent patrol. It also states that 'vast improvement[s] in current strategic conditions since the end of the Cold War also permit [the Royal Navy] to adopt a reduced day-to-day alert state.'

The general hope is that the Royal Navy has one Vanguard-class submarine at sea, one being repaired, one in dock, and one ready to go out (or out in addition to the one already at sea). This constant rotation enables maintenance to fit into a rota, and the 160-strong crews to rotate through patrol, downtime, and onshore duties. The crew is thoroughly trained through a scheme known as SMQ, or Submariner Qualification, in which potential submariners undergo submarine-specific training in a classroom on land, before heading off with a submarine to finish their training books onboard. They then have to pass a test in front of a board of qualified submariners, in which they answer questions about everything and anything onboard.[20] A pass means they get their dolphins – a badge submariners wear proudly to show they are qualified and a member of

19 This is available to view online. I signed the Official Secrets Act, and to be honest am unsure how much I can and can't reveal about the Royal Navy Submarine Service. Therefore I will err on the side of caution and only include information that is publicly available.
20 These phases are called SMQ Dry and SMQ Wet.

the Royal Navy Submarine Service. Each submarine is stocked with three months' worth of food and then the crew head off.[21]

This, however, does not mean mistakes are avoided. The crew may be very prepared and extremely well educated, but these underwater behemoths have had their fair share of incidents:

HMS Vanguard collision with Le Triomphant: Between the 3rd and 4th February 2009, the Royal Navy's Vanguard submarine collided with the French Navy's Le Triomphant. Initially the French Ministry of Defence believed their submarine had collided with a large submerged object, while the UK Ministry of Defence refused to acknowledge the incident altogether. HMS Vanguard then, whilst carrying Trident nuclear missiles, took damage to the outer casing in the area of the missile compartment. William McNeilly described the incident in rather shocking terms, implying that the submarine was so heavily damaged that it could've sunk to the bottom of the ocean had one of the loosened high pressured air bottle groups exploded.

Radioactive Cooling Waters: In 2014 it was reported that low levels of radioactivity had been discovered in the cooling water of a nuclear submarine test reactor at Dounreay. This, however, was discovered in 2012, and kept quiet from the public, or even opposition parties – as Labour suggested it was a matter

---

21 The food is pretty great. I guess it depends on the chef and logistics, but I never had a bad meal while on board.

of national importance, and the government had failed to announce this issue. The defence secretary at the time, Philip Hammond, stated that there was no detectable radiation leak, and 'these low levels of radioactivity are a normal product of a nuclear reaction that takes place within the fuel'. He did however concede that such reactions 'would not normally enter the cooling water.'

William McNeilly's[22] *Claims:* William McNeilly in his dossier, suggested that the Vanguard-class submarines barely worked, and there were running jokes onboard that Trident was so poorly maintained that it wouldn't work should a situation ever require it. His accounts were a smorgasbord of defective equipment, uncaring crew, and lax security checks. McNeilly claimed that he had repeatedly tried to bring his concerns to individuals within the Submarine Service, and had been ignored time and time again – leading him to feel that he had no choice but to make his claims public.[23]

Failed Trident Missile Test: In June 2016, an unarmed Trident II D5 ballistic missile was testfired off the coast of Florida. This missile, weighing 60 tonnes and with the capability to produce eight times the devastation of Hiroshima, was intended to follow a

---

22 William McNeilly is a Royal Navy Submarine Service whistleblower. He went AWOL from the Navy and gave large amounts of secret information and classified information to news sources. He was eventually arrested and apprehended. Any and all information presented are his accounts, are publicly available, and may or may not be verified by the Ministry of Defence.

23 Again, all this information is available online and is the account of William McNeilly alone.

set path, and – at a cost of £17m – provide a successful test and reassure the Royal Navy of its nuclear deterrent. This did not happen. The missile veered seven thousand miles off course and instead of heading towards the southern Atlantic it began to occupy the sky above the US. The test was aborted without damage and kept quiet for a full six months before being revealed to the public or parliament. Theresa May was informed about the test and subsequently chose not to inform MPs, a heavily criticised decision. This was particularly concerning as the test failure happened one month before a House of Commons vote on the next generation of Trident – it was widely believed that Theresa May had kept the failure under wraps to ensure the vote passed without incident. With these incidents and failures accounting for just a small amount of the problems the Royal Navy Submarine Service has encountered, it begs the question whether the UK's submarines are in a position to carry Trident missiles, and whether the programme can be deemed safe or secure at all. The Vanguards cost a total of £15 billion – considering the need for more money in the NHS[24] as just one small example, is it really necessary to spend so much on a service that can be argued to be faulty, prone to error, and carrying up to 16 weapons capable of devastation regardless of whether they hit their target or not?

---

24 Never mind the Leave campaign's £350m lie about funding the NHS.

Trident replaced Polaris as the Royal Navy's missile system in 1994, and is currently active as 40 warheads and 8 missiles spread across the 4 Vanguard-class submarines. Targets can be reached from 7,500 miles. When a Trident missile leaves the submarine, a rocket ignites and the aerospike is extended. A sequence then occurs in which a first and second stage rocket are ignited and then jettisoned in order, before the warheads eject from a third stage rocket. The warheads are individually and independently released and free fall to a target upon which they detonate.

It has been estimated that the cost of renewing Trident for operational deployment in the 2030s could exceed £97 billion.[25] This could provide for 150,000 new nurses and teachers every year until 2047, overcoming the strain in the NHS and our education services – crises that will surely be worsened if Brexit causes the departure of EU nationals that these services rely upon. The money could also fund all accident and emergency services in UK hospitals beyond 2057, or build 1.5 million affordable homes, or pay the tuition fees for 4 million students. Arguments for the renewal of Trident include the 7,000 jobs created by its renewal, yet this fails to account for the potential 2,000,000 jobs that could be created should the money be used elsewhere.[26]

Most Trident supporters would suggest that the safety of the UK is dependent on having a continuous at-sea nuclear deterrent on patrol, and that

25 Estimated by Greenpeace, but the Campaign for Nuclear Disarmament estimates replacing Trident could cost at least £205 billion.
26 A lot of this information comes from the Campaign for Nuclear Disarmament, as well as other news sources such as *The Guardian*, and *The Independent*.

other countries may not attack if they believe they would be at risk of retaliation. Essentially, the argument suggests that we go down fighting, and blow up as much of the world as possible before we are blown up ourselves. Yet this argument provides its own counterpoint, as it becomes clear that countries have nuclear weapons because of the nuclear potential of each other, that the world is a more dangerous place because it is deemed necessary to have a retaliation against somebody else's retaliation. It is also important to note that the majority of issues are not on such a big scale as to require nuclear attacks – Britain is struggling to feed and shelter its homeless as food banks spiral out of control and thousands go without warm homes.[27] On a global scale, these problems persist, as Syrian refugees beg for aid they are not receiving, safe water becomes more and more of a scarcity, and landmines maim thousands a year. UN peacekeeping forces require £5 billion a year, and the UN Development Programme is budgeted at £3 billion – a small amount compared to the ever increasing costs of Trident renewal.[28]

With the potential for financial distribution to other, more necessary programs, it becomes increasingly hard to argue for the expensive renewal of Trident. It instead acts a status symbol for Britain, a show of power for a country that has no need for such heavy weaponry where conventional and smaller-scale defence would suffice. It is clear that

---

27 Which puts more strain on the already underfunded NHS.
28 As footnote 26.

a system so prone to error, so dangerous, and so costly is no longer needed in this modern age – if it was ever needed at all. The final say on this subject should be given over to the International Court of Justice, who ruled in 1996 that the use of nuclear weapons is illegal and contrary to international law. Illegal, costly, and unsafe – what is the argument to keep Trident?

Aaron Kent is a screenwriter and poet from Cornwall. He served in the Royal Navy as a Sonar Submariner (Warfare Specialist) from 2009-2012. He now lectures in poetry, and film. He and his wife are preparing to welcome their first baby. Aaron wishes there were more poems about Godzilla.

THE NATIONS/ REGIONS

LONDON: THE CURIOUS CASE OF SLIPPERY ZAC

by Kavita A. Jindal

The call to power is a siren song. I've been collecting election campaign leaflets since 2004, and it makes for an interesting game to compare old and new leaflets from candidates to see how they change; how they flip-flop in a bid to pursue power.

In my borough of Richmond Park we are presented with the remarkable case of Zac Goldsmith. When he stood as an 'independent' candidate in the Richmond by-election in December 2016, the only question many of us had was: win or lose, how long before he re-joins the Conservative Party?

That question is answered now: Four months.

So far, so predictable.

Even the opposition statement: 'He doesn't have a shred of credibility', is predictable. But it's true. For those in the borough un-swayed by the thought of low taxes and by Zac's good looks there hasn't been a shred of credibility in the man since before the last general election. His political trajectory, explained below, illustrates why.

He became our MP in 2010 when, as a Conservative candidate, he defeated the incumbent Liberal Democrat candidate. At the time, there was not much difference between the parties on local issues – they all campaigned on 'no Heathrow expansion',

'Health/NHS', and 'local services.'

In October 2009, David Cameron, tipped to be the next prime minister, made a personal pledge during a visit to a school in Richmond that there would be no third runway at Heathrow – 'no ifs, no buts'. This boosted Zac's chances and the Tories locally as this was the burning issue for residents. And perhaps many were running scared of the proposed 'mansion tax' touted by the Lib Dems.

As an MP in his first run, Zac was a popular figure.

He stood again when the next general election was announced in 2015. There was never any doubt that he would win. However, the Conservative Party's 'green façade' was slipping. In May 2010 the slogan had been 'vote blue, go green'. In fact, Cameron had pledged the 'greenest government ever'. (Perhaps we shouldn't mention any of Cameron's pledges, as they seem not to have held up).

Environmentalists had started to point out that Tory politics did not match the stated policies. There were worries that in the event of a Conservative majority environmentally-friendly policies would be killed off (which is exactly what happened; but that's a separate essay).

Zac was actively campaigning in the constituency. About two months before the election date I met him at an event organised for local women by the Women's Institute. I went along out of curiosity despite not being a member of WI. Two things happened that evening. A lady who must've been distressed (as most people were) at the news reports of a group of Rochdale taxi drivers in court for their criminal offences of grooming and abusing vulnerable girls, asked him: 'Shouldn't all Pakistani taxi drivers be deported? They shouldn't be allowed to drive taxis.' 'Er…' said Zac.

'*All* Pakistani drivers,' she repeated. She said a few other things in that mode. Suffice to say that Zac couldn't find it in himself to be fair and to answer reasonably that perhaps all ethnic-origin Pakistani drivers shouldn't be tarred with the Rochdale brush. Because presumably not all white, male, English television personalities are paedophiles.

All Zac did was acknowledge the lady each time, and plead with the discomfited audience for other questions. The lady continued to push him. She repeated her views, very strongly and clearly. She wanted a loud and uncompromising sign of his agreement with her, which was difficult for him, of course, so he ended up tacitly letting her get away with her remarks. This was a single vote that Zac didn't want to lose and it was clear that he would let racist and extreme views pass if he found them in his support group. I can also add that the audience in the room was not particularly diverse (which reflects the constituency) and that to my knowledge, there was not a single ethnic-origin Pakistani in the room. Still, I was extremely disappointed in that moment.

Zac's talk had been full of how different he was from the others at Westminster. Well, same difference, I thought. Slippery politician.

At this meeting Zac also stressed his environmental credentials and how he had once been the 'preferred' candidate of the Green Party. He insisted that he was the most committed candidate on environmental issues. Listening to him differentiate himself again, and hearing him declare 'I am a politician of principle' got me thinking. On the subject of Heathrow expansion, he was in a strong position. It wasn't on the cards – then. He had a good record locally and there was nothing the other candidates could offer that he couldn't. Unless you had an interest in environmental policies. Whatever Zac's personal values, the Conservatives seemed to be rolling back from their 'greenest party' ideas. The future didn't look encouraging in that aspect.

I raised my hand to enquire how Zac squared being a Tory at the same time as championing environment-friendly policies. Weren't the Conservatives slowly dismantling any green agenda they may have had?

'Your principles and your politics don't match,' I commented. He replied that he was a committed environmentalist. 'In that case, aren't you in the wrong party?' I asked. I didn't think the Greens had a shot at winning in Richmond but Zac almost had it in the bag because of his massive popularity. 'Why don't you stand as an independent?' I suggested.

Zac put his hand on his heart to reply in that overwrought sincere manner he adopts, which incidentally, causes him to look insincere. 'I am a Conservative. I will *always* be a Conservative.' All who attended the WI meeting on 5th March 2015 at the Bull's Head pub bore witness to this.

It was no great surprise that on a campaign promise that he would resign if ever there was the go-ahead for a third runway at Heathrow, he kept his seat in May 2015, with an increased majority of 23,015. Great result for Zac.

Exactly one year later he was competing to be the Mayor of London. He was the Conservative candidate and the party had delayed a decision on airport expansion until after the mayoral election to help his chances.

During this campaign Zac sent a letter to 'British Indians', as he termed them in the mailshot. His team must have trawled through the electoral roll to identify individuals whose surnames sounded Hindu and those people received a specific leaflet as well as a letter exclusively addressed to them from David Cameron.

Plenty more on that letter and leaflet coming up but I just want to digress here. I would love to hear from the person(s) whose job it was to tick off those names on the London electoral roll. Please, get in touch. I am curious about so much.

I've dug out the mailshot to re-read it and here are some choice excerpts:

Sadiq Khan, Zac's rival for Mayor, is referred to as 'radical'.

We're to fill in the blank ourselves as in: radical what? Radical about what?

Just 'radical' as in 'cool'? Somehow I don't think they meant that.

Perhaps this is just code for 'Muslim'. Thanks, Zac, for pointing this out.

Are we meant to hate Sadiq for being born into that religion? Perhaps his surname 'Khan' should warn us off voting for him. Because no Muslim-sounding surnames are receiving this letter, are they? Even when they too, are, 'British Indian'. What about 'British Indian' Christians? Did you select them for this letter? I have my doubts, but what do I know?

Zac's own nephews have the Muslim surname 'Khan'. (His sister, Jemima, was married to the Pakistani cricketer-turned-politician Imran Khan). Despite that he failed to recognise the inherent prejudice in this leaflet. What does that tell us about him?

The leaflet also pointed out that Sadiq Khan's party 'SUPPORTS A WEALTH TAX on family jewellery' (not my capitals, but Zac's). I'm not averse to hoarding family jewellery; on the contrary, I believe in it, because I adore the pieces of old jewellery I've inherited from relatives who are now long-dead. And because it means you can touch and treasure something that remains as it was from the time your great-grand-mother wore it. But I can't tell you how much this point riled me. Should I be deciding whom to vote for as London Mayor based on the loose suggestion that Labour wants to tax British Indians on the gold they like to accumulate? Thanks for the stereotype and also for letting us know which issues we should prioritise.

The leaflet goes on to say that 'Sadiq Khan won't be able to work with the Government'. Well, all I can say is, we know that Zac will be able to work with the government; he *has* been working with the government while it merrily cuts green policies. The leaflet tells us that 'Zac has a strong record of engagement with the Indian community celebrating Diwali, Navratri and Janmashtami.' Glad to know that Zac celebrates more Hindu festivals than I do. Someone in his team believes they know what we want to hear. Clearly this homogenous huge 'British Indian' community of London doesn't celebrate Muslim festivals (if you go by the leaflet). Nor Sikh. The community also only cares about our 'family owned businesses' (quote from the leaflet) and Hinduism; and being prejudiced against other religions (although India has devotees of seven religions, at least, at last count). Because here is a photograph of Zac and Cameron buddying up to the visiting Indian Prime Minister Narendra Modi (while Sadiq is featured next to an unpopular Jeremy Corbyn).

Yeah, right. Sending me a photo of you hugging Modi will make me back you.

I heard that using this photo completely backfired. I wasn't the only person aghast at this pandering to Hindu extremism and the cynical melding of Indian politics into the London mayoral election.

London is in the UK, Zac; hope you've noticed. Leave Modi out of it.

Did I say the vile mailshot properly did the job of making me feel 'other'?

Did my family not care about transport in London, clean air, the environment, and affordable housing for the workers of London: the people who make this wonderful city tick? No, apparently we only cared about amassing jewellery, low taxes for our houses and businesses, and being anti-Muslim. It could be that Zac's letter appealed to a percentage of the targeted voting group; perhaps the same percentage as that elderly English lady at the WI meeting, who held similar views. Just from another perspective. It could be that the mailshot to the 'Hindus of London' was a clever strategy. But that he would stoop to it was heartbreaking.

Most Londoners are liberal people. Even 'British Indians'. We've all seen enough divide and rule nonsense in the Indian sub-continent and we're all aware of rising religious intolerance everywhere. Inciting or supporting the flames of hatred towards any one group is a recipe for disaster.

It was too bad that the mainstream press (with a few usual exceptions) barely reported Zac's bilious mail-out. Most of my neighbours in the constituency had no clue. Nor did many of my friends. Some people in Richmond didn't believe me until I produced the four letters we received (to the four people in our household who share the same last name). After he lost the mayoral election, some of his supporters and family made excuses for this hateful campaigning. Apparently, it wasn't Zac's idea. Not how he would have campaigned. No? That's his signature on the letters. He signed off on the plan. Incidentally, a similar mailshot was sent to 'London Tamils', tailored specifically for them. It may have been Lynton Crosby and others at No. 10 who suggested and masterminded the strategy (we don't know), but where was Zac's brain? Perhaps it was working out the meaning of 'principled'.

Golden Zac was badly tarnished. But he still had his MP duties and status. In June 2016 the EU referendum vote resulted in an 'out' result. Zac was always a Brexit man. His father founded the Referendum Party and Zac has said in interviews that he didn't believe in the case for remaining in Europe. Yet he didn't have the guts to campaign loudly for this set of principles. Richmond-upon-Thames had an 82% turnout for the EU referendum and 69.3% voted to stay in the EU. Zac was not in sync with his constituents on that score, and he tried to stay quiet about it.

In October 2016, the Heathrow consortium lobbyists got the result they wanted when the government approved a third runway, paving the way for hundreds of thousands more flights a year over West London.

On this, his major campaign point, Zac has been completely ineffectual within the Tory party. They don't take him seriously. He resigned when the runway was approved because he says that unlike other politicians, he 'keeps his word'. Considering his promise to resign was prominent on numerous pieces of literature he'd sent during his election campaign he had no choice. On resigning, he could have gone on to fight on this issue as a common citizen, using his money and his might. But that's not what happened. Zac Goldsmith stood as an 'independent' candidate in the by-election triggered by his resignation from the Conservative Party.

He asked us to vote him in again as our MP. The local Conservative office didn't put up a candidate against him. UKIP gave him its stamp of approval. Although Zac hoped that Richmond residents would forget the salient fact that he was in favour of Brexit. He was not 'representative' of the constituency any more in any form.

Last October I was puzzled, to say the least. Hand-on-heart Zac the forever Tory, standing as an independent to remain in power. This is also the man who said that he didn't 'need' Westminster like some politicians did. But he couldn't let go, could he?

The Lib Dems threw everything they had into that by-election in December 2016 and Sarah Olney scraped a narrow win over Zac. The only question in my mind when he lost was the same one as when he'd declared himself an 'independent': How long now before he crawls back to the Tory tent? We now know the answer: Four months.

As I write he's secured the Conservative nomination for the constituency. He's been allowed another lunge at power. The fact that he's unimpressive and unheeded at Westminster seems not to matter to the Richmond Conservative office. They know his massive fan base eclipses any other local Conservative candidate. Perhaps voters will see no wrong in him, or forgive his Brexit 'lapse'. The racially-divisive leaflets don't matter to the Conservatives; it's part of their agenda, after all.

In fact, calling this snap election is a sure-fire way to escalate the nasty rhetoric and lies of the EU referendum. No doubt we will hear hatred spewing again: against Europeans, eastern Europeans, all immigrants, anybody foreign, anybody not English… a silly indefinable list but one that the right-wing thrives on. Although many of them can't quite quantify their own background (but that's another essay).

Meanwhile I quote from the high-quality full-colour four-page newsletter Zac sent out last October. Title of the piece: 'Stronger as an Independent MP.' From the text: 'As an Independent MP, Zac will be a critical friend to the Government supporting it on measures that he believes are in the best interest of the constituency, and holding them to account on the issues that are not.'

For Zac 'being critical' and 'holding to account' must be synonymous with 're-joining'.

Forgive me while I struggle to understand how re-joining the Conservative Party gives him an edge over anyone or anything. Granted it gives him the Conservative vote-bloc: people who vote Conservative, no matter what. So all those mailshots that assured me he was 'Stronger As An Independent' amount to nothing. How can Zac explain his 'broken promise' of independence and his lack of a plan on 'holding to account' his party on environmental policy? How green is Zac's heart?

I am curious to see what spin his next leaflet (yet to be received at the time of going to press) will put on his actions. Can there really be an excuse for the indefensible? Who will buy it?

As an uncompromising Brexit supporter who's now courting the votes of 'Remainers', the majority in his constituency, I detect some squeamishness in telling the truth. When interviewed he tries to evade mentioning how strongly he was for 'Out of the EU'. Zac says that he 'understands the rage' people in the borough feel, but now Brexit is on the horizon and 'only Theresa May can properly deliver it'.

What he's really saying to his constituents is: I'm not sorry for anything, but I want you to vote for me. Let me be your MP at any cost. Ignore my failures. Ignore my party affiliation and non-affiliation. It's all the same.

The media says he has an uphill task, but I would wager he has a good chance.

What I can't see is how he can style himself 'a politician of principle'.

Not many humans can withstand an addiction to power. I understand. Honesty falls away, naturally, as it's dangerous for politicians to speak the truth. The loss of principles is standard too, but less remarked on. There should be more weight given to it.

For my part, my wish is that no candidate standing in London ever uses racial profiling the way Zac Goldsmith did in the mayoral race. Such campaigning destroys what makes London a special place: in my mind, socially and culturally, London is the most advanced city in the world.

No thanks to Zac.

He, of all people, should know better.

If I hark back to this it's because it hurts me that it should be my MP at the time who perpetrated such a divisive smear-filled campaign. He can never regain credibility.

In approximately a month from the time of writing, we shall know if the polite populace of Richmond have once again elected the disingenuous Zac Goldsmith to represent them. All will be clear on June 9th.

Kavita A. Jindal is a prize-winning fiction writer, as well as a poet, essayist and reviewer. She is the author of Raincheck Renewed, *published to critical acclaim by Chameleon Press. She is the co-founder of The Whole Kahani collective and a Senior Editor at* Asia Literary Review.

NORTHERN IRELAND: AN UNHOLY MARRIAGE

by Michael Wilson

Throughout Northern Irish politics there is a flavour of the will being strong but the flesh being weak. This is also a country riven with division – socially, between the two communities (Protestant and Catholic) that co-habit the small province, and politically because the power of sectarianism informs so much grass roots opinion on hot potato topics such as same sex marriage or the role of the Gaelic language. These divisions speak loudest in the case of cross-community power sharing (which seems a solution in theory, but proves more than unwieldy in practice) – Northern Ireland is made up of red lines, ideological jargon and a sense that the province is so far behind the times you'd believe it was frozen in time, one week before the release of 'Love Me Do'.

Why? It's simple: because of the unholy alliance or marriage between church and state. To understand Northern Ireland at all is to realise that Theresa May's own Bible-bashing is the lightest of light touches compared to the sheer evangelical approach of Arlene Foster, the leader – for now – of the DUP (Democratic Unionist Party). The DUP are the largest party at Stormont (although by only one seat). Upon taking the job as First Leader of the Stormont assembly, Foster asserted that the DUP are a Christian (read, Protestant) party and are there to make the province work as a Christian state.

This very fact, or rather, worldview, was revealed to me during a discussion I had with a DUP MLA as a representative for the Ethnic Minorities Empowerment Association. I proposed to the politician that surely to create and encourage cultural and ethnic togetherness and unity, we should have schools cover at least an overview of other religions alternative to Christianity. The MLA looked at me like I had just come in from the last tide. The DUP MLA stated that Ulster (Northern Ireland) is a Christian province and a Christian state. I didn't need to argue the first of that, although even Ulster has seen drops in church attendance, but the second is a contentious point. In the echo chambers of Facebook and other social media platforms, among the 'right-on' thinking liberals, centrists and leftists, you'll find many that have not only turned their backs on religion, but highlight the marriage of church and state as as much to blame for the state of government these days as the infamous top 1% of British society.

Worringly, if the main parties were to successfully power share and find harmony and efficiency in the running of Stormont, the tribal voting and electoral posturing that keeps so many MLAs in jobs would shift and diminish, and those MLAs might find themselves without a mandate. Their ethos seems to be to divide and carve up rather than conquer; to keep the home fires burning and keep the working class Catholics and Protestants from working out that they have more in common with each other than their tribal political elites.

As for North and South, 1.85 million vehicles cross the border per year, with a huge chunk of them lorries and trucks (nearly 300,000 per annum). The psychological effect of the old border checkpoints are something that seemed to be a relic, but now with Brexit, where do the checks come in? Is it a hard or soft border? The Irish government are, as we speak, working out where border points will be less problematic for businesses for both sides, such as at seaports and airports rather than on roads. It quickly appears that Brexit is a worse deal for the Northern Irish than for the English, and indeed the Northern Irish clearly felt so, with 56 per cent voting to remain in the EU.

Here, however, things get increasingly tribal. Unionists (despite splits) were largely pro-Brexit (since Unionists tend to shadow the Tories' stance on issues) and the nationalists, republicans and Alliance (a middle ground party) all voted to remain. With this election being trumpeted by May as about Brexit, this is an issue that divides again, even as some elements are trying (a little too desperately) to create a cross-community anti-Brexit alliance. Ann Travers, whose sister Mary was killed by the IRA, states that in her opinion, the SDLP (Social Democratic Labour Party), the main nationalist party, will have to get into bed with the republican Sinn Féin, currently the second-biggest party in Northern Ireland. Travers believes that if this happens, the SDLP will lose nationalist voters, since Sinn Féin had a history of being joined at the hip with the IRA paramilitaries during the Troubles and still fail to condone the IRA's violent past. It would appear that in Northern Ireland, people have longer memories than a herd of elephants in a MENSA meeting. The shadow over Northern Ireland shows how slowly things seem to be moving, while a huge watershed moment seems to be sweeping the province: that of rising republicanism under Sinn Féin.

As a child of the Troubles I never saw politics as something that could ever deliver on its promises. On the radio in the family car (a Datsun) the phrase 'tit for tat' was something I was exposed to very early. The paramilitary 'eye for an eye' was a horrendous loop of violence that carried on throughout the latter part of the 20th century; once the IRA had murdered a Protestant, the Loyalist paramilitaries would strike back by murdering a Catholic. Tit for tat – its intractability its chain of deaths, each echoing the past one – seemed like a maddening wheel that no one was able to get off. These days, though, the paramilitaries are involved in criminal, not political targets. Sinn Féin, once a party of extremes as the loudspeaker for the IRA, is now second to the DUP by only one seat. Its rise to such standing is almost boy's own territory for their greatest supporters, and shows Northern Ireland's ability to cope with change.

To understand the present in Northern Ireland, we are doomed to view its past. That seemingly gloomy and ghoulish vista has shown the importance of forgiveness in Northern Ireland. This is where the marriage of state and church might suggest a helping hand – after all what's better suited to Christian mores than forgiveness? It is as much a credit to Sinn Féin that they can not only bring about the agreed decommissioning of weapons, join in power sharing and work well in Stormont on the issues of education, health and the budget, as much as to those in the electorate that made them the second biggest party in Northern Ireland and secured them the position of Deputy First Minister to the leader. It would appear that the people of Northern Ireland can forgive if not forget. However, for all the shine of Sinn Féin replacing the SDLP's position as the main Catholic-supported party, there is still no way that many in the Protestant communities would ever vote nationalist or republican, except tactically to keep out Sinn Féin. The times, they are a-changing. That's why the old dragon head of tribal, religious and political posturing is the lifeblood of the DUP – with the working classes feeling more and more alienated, the only way the DUP can keep Sinn Féin out is to continue marrying politics and religion. Indeed, the province can arguably be seen as following Karl Marx's belief that religion is the opium of the masses.

The fact remains that the working classes and underclasses of Northern Ireland on each side of the peace wall have more in common with each other than the elite ideologue politicians that serve to keep them at bay and out of touch with each other, for fear they will realise that in Northern Ireland, politics is served with a bastardisation of religion, a religion that splits brothers and sisters up and leaders apart. The religious state is like the lazy writers of second rate comedy sitcoms, barely even trying to go beyond the obvious, failing to push any kind of envelope with punchlines that groan into view – and that's when the parties can even be bothered to work together.

The DUP's most conservative Christian wing, personified by Peter Weir, argues that same sex marriage will split the DUP and will not lift a veto on debating on it or voting for it. To block the bill the DUP need 30 MLAs to agree to a petition of concern (something supposedly there to protect minority interests) as it offends their religious freedoms. Currently, they are 2 MLAs short, so they will make a pact with the one TUV MLA and a conservative independent member. It seems sickening that something like a petition of concern be used by the majority to protect the Christian Province from itself, when it was originally there to protect minorities. It recalls the House Un-American Activities Committee, and how it grew out of a fear of fascism with the aim of protecting liberal rights, then ended up a weapon of the right in America to punish the left. In Northern Ireland, however, both sides of the political die have abused the petition of concern.

The republicans also have their red line, and that is the leadership of Arlene Foster. Foster was in charge of a project to encourage burning more sustainable fuel (in pellets); the farmers and businesses that signed up found that they received a payment for burning the fuel that amounted to more than its actual cost. The maths were so bad that they actually made money through the scheme. The project was abused by many, and the mistake cost the Northern Irish coffers almost 500 million pounds. In the wake of this scandal, the republicans refuse to start power sharing until Arlene Foster steps down, at least until the inquiry into the scandal has been conducted.

Ellis O'Hanlon for the *Belfast Telegraph* has pointed out that this whole issue, which was why Stormont fell apart in the first place, is perhaps no longer the driving seat of how the parties are debating the world around them. O'Hanlon believes that Sinn Féin are instead itching to raise the possibility of a border poll and therefore a united Ireland. In the past, such a wish was just that, a wish – but today, with the main republican party almost neck and neck with the main unionist party, everyone should be aware of the potential size of this issue.

As for Sinn Féin, the main reason they can't make government work at Stormont is their attempts to woo the South of Ireland, currently governed by an anti-austerity party. Sinn Féin, therefore, cannot be seen to accept and work with austerity budgets in the north and so despite the failures of the other parties at keeping Stormont active, Sinn Féin are as much to blame as their rivals.

So what, apart from religious divides, are the main positions of the parties after the announcement of the election in June?

Unlike Labour in England, some components of the main parties are voicing this election as a possibility to lobby a pro-European group into Westminster. But as already stated, the religious divide seems to be halting the appeal of an alliance outside of nationalist parties. The DUP and UUP (Ulster Unionist Party) are arguing about whether to run a unionist pact in Belfast South to keep out the SDLP MP Alasdair McDonnell, the most cynical of tactical voting. But what has come out of the blue is Arlene Foster agreeing to meet POBAL, a Gaelic language advocacy group, that she doesn't see or label as hyper-political. It would seem that what was once a red line for Unionists, the promotion of Gaelic in Northern Ireland, could be possible. Such developments offer hope.

What could happen as a result of the national election? Firstly, most of the Northern Irish MPs in Westminster will be pro-Europe but divided outside that very issue. Sinn Féin will battle strongly for a bigger mandate in the national election, building on their rise as it stands at Stormont. However, due to the long-running boycott of the Palace of Westminster, they will not actually physically be there. The SDLP might be wary of going into an alliance with Sinn Féin, not just because of this but because a major raison d'être of larger Northern Irish parties is gobbling up smaller ones. The SDLP and

UUP have a strange place in recent history – the two more moderate parties were once upon a time the leading forces for nationalists and unionists, and as such brokered the peace. Bizarrely it was the DUP that marched and protested against the Good Friday Agreement talks, so much has changed, yet little at the same time.

In Northern Ireland, little gets by without a sectarian spin, or at least a question of how it relates to the marriage of religion and the state. Politics was once a subject for the dinner table but not the bar. The province now enjoys relative prosperity – even in these economically troubled times it has the big fat jewel in its crown of tourism and leisure, not least driven by *Game of Thrones*, Hollywood film shoots and also the new(ish) Titanic Centre. The word 'cosmopolitan' has even been heard floating across the river in Londonderry/Derry. Even the Troubles themselves are now an entertaining sideshow in Belfast, with black cab drivers conducting tours of historical hotspots. The mural tradition is alive and well, but either as an old curio or as inspiration for new street art murals that are fervently political in their apolitical subject matter. You could be anywhere, in any city.

Northern Ireland could work very well, if it had an assembly that acted pragmatically and without breaking down whenever they perceived a bill as an erosion of power or position. It can be argued that the present stalemate has more to do with traditional unionists enjoying precious little assistance at a grass roots level, especially in relation to Sinn Féin in the same provision.

This is not a simple regional problem that exists on its own. Across the west, working class sectors are becoming more extreme, with the middle ground losing its way since the great experiments in social democratic and conservative right-tinged power across Europe and America. In France, perfectly sane individuals are favouring Le Pen. English working classes vote for UKIP. Americans elected a caricature of big business as president. It seems no one cares much about Northern Ireland – if they did there wouldn't be a general election at such a difficult time. Also, the impression is that James Brokenshire (Conservative Secretary of State for Northern Ireland) would rather he gets a favourable reshuffle after June's general election.

So, what about direct rule? If the Stormont parties can't broker a deal to re-enter the assembly by the end of June, direct rule (rule by Westminster, the end of devolution) will be enacted. There are some advantages to this: sticky bills such as the budget will sail through. Direct rule will also give the opportunity to steer the entire politics of Northern Ireland into wider debates than the provincial opinions of Stormont MLAs. In contrast, the downsides would include the threat of increased paramilitary attacks from dissident republican groups with a focus on anti-direct rule. It is worth noting that barely anyone seems to be favouring these dissident groups and are far from accepting their sporadic violence, yet during the opening years of the Troubles the popularity of the IRA was virtually nil. Whatever happens, the impression is that Theresa May has other issues at heart in this Brexit-influenced election.

Once again it appears the Conservative government has pulled a rug from under a lot of people who have voted and voted and voted, and for what? A lot of blaming each other, and not much in the way of anything concrete. Until the divorce of church and state things won't change quickly, which may become something for future generations to see to. There are some people already who are of voting age in Northern Ireland who were born after the Good Friday Agreement. With the next generation, Northern Ireland has an opportunity to put to bed the spectre of the Troubles, that in the early peace of these times still influences so much. In some regards, few have come as far as Northern Ireland – its present was once undreamt of – but even with devolution in stasis and crisis talks dead in the water, it could be worse, and the population is never far from reflecting on that.

Michael Wilson has a BA degree in History and Politics and an MA in History. He is a performance poet who specialises in highlighting and increasing awareness of disability. He resides in Portstewart, a town in Northern Ireland, and runs poetry events.

WALES

by Ben Gwalchmai

April 21st, 2017 – I'm in Ribamar, Portugal, having eaten too many crisps and enjoyed way more sun than any Welshman expects, supposed to be holiday-ing and thinking of nothing but relaxing... yet Wales is on my mind. *You are always on my mind, you are al-ways on my mind...*Wales, that is – not you. My 'you', our 'you' – see, you can take the boyo out of Wales but you can't take Wales out the boi (we're still sur-prised that Zeta-Jones and Anthony Hopkins haven't come back. Give them time, mind).

Jokes aside, Wales has a strong cultural iden-tity and a strong pull for those of us who grew up there. This is not necessarily by state means: Wales has only had the opportunity to teach its own his-tory in schools since 1997. Take that in for a second: a country's entire history was taught only outside of schools for generations. Even after that, it's only been 20 years. Wales has only been allowed to make its own laws, teach its own history – to understand itself – for 20 years. Notice the wording there, 'al-lowed to'; that's because in the first iteration of the Senedd (a.k.a. the Welsh Assembly), Wales would request laws and London could deign to give them or tell them to jog on. Britain's Empire built a long, callous shadow that the whole of the UK is still to emerge from.

And here the UK is, in AlmostBrexitland – the wet dream of retired colonels, millionaires, press barons, people too young to have fought in WW2 but old enough to have forgotten that life was surprisingly good after rationing, people too privileged to give a rat's arse, people who bought the lies of all the preceding people, etc. Because of the Empire.

Before we can hazard a guess at what Wales' #GE2017 might hold, we need to understand the contemporary state of Wales shackled to Almost-Brexitland as it is and we need to know why it narrowly (yes, narrowly) voted Leave in the EU referendum. So let's make sure you're up to speed, shall we?

In 500AD, an old form of the Welsh language was spoken across the majority of (what's now) England and Wales. Surprising, I know, but true: ask the historian Grant Allen who included a map of the languages spoken on the British Isles in his book *Anglo-Saxon Britain*.

1066 and all that… happened. Kingdoms fell by the swordside or were married into oblivion. The medieval history of Wales gets even murkier and more fertile than the language's fall from its heights. Much blood fell, lands bore the brunt of ill boots, lords rose, roses sang; say all that in an epic-fantasy voice and you get a rose-tinted picture of roughly 200 years.

In 1277 and 1283, Edward the First took on the Welsh and won. 1283 was Wales' first death. Even then though, Wales operated under different laws. Wales was hereafter known as 'The Principality of Wales'.

Wales' second death came in 1415, when the Glyndŵr Rising fell. With allegiances sworn between Breton, Scotland, and France, Owain Glyndŵr fought a good fight, taking back all of Wales and then some. Unfortunately, things fell apart politically, militarily, and economically. Those 15 years were the last time Wales was an independent country.

Plenty of privileged, jingoistic people still call Wales 'The Principality' and I would gladly punch all of these people in the face if only the Welsh Arts Council would accept my application. This is because their understanding of history is... potted. At best. Wales hasn't been a principality since the 1535 'Laws in Wales Acts' which – put simply – made Welsh and English law the same. Our language has endured oppression but a section in this act was the beginning of it in earnest.

That particular section of the act was refuted in – put your glass down because you might just drop it – 1993. Yes, *1993*.

Yes, I've triple checked. Some argue 1887 saw a slight repeal but considering the Welsh Not, you can bet your ass that the damn thing was still there culturally. So: that's 458 years where Welsh was legally oppressed. Much like colonies in the British Empire.

Apart from the post-1997 devolution period, that brings you up to speed. Oh, sure, I could tell you about the birth of the NHS (forged by Aneurin Bevan, a Welshman) or Chartism as the seed for socialism, that Everest is named after its Welsh surveyor or that a Welshman invented the equals sign (yes, '=' is Welsh); I could even go on to tell you that Wales is the only part of the UK not represented on the Union Jack flag but I figure you already knew all that; after all, how would a country that's full of so much history not get taught to its neighbours? I was taught English history in school and European history at A Level but I was never taught Welsh, were you? If so, please email me and tell me where you went so I can tell my sister to send her unborn children there. If not, why not?

Ah yes, that sticky thing: the Empire. I blame a lot on it, don't I? Likely because the Victorian era invented 'Britishness' in its current, Boris Johnson as Jack Bull, unwieldy, arrogant, human rights-denying form.

All of this might read like I've a giant chip on my shoulder. Well: you're underestimating its size, it's humongous. This also might read like I'm angry... and I am. When it comes to Wales' place in the UK, I am pissed off... but that means I'm fired up too.

April 23rd, 2017 —
I am staring Freedom of Movement down. The EU will bend to my will. I am successful, I am powerful, I am strong and stable. I will achieve my goal of a tax-haven UK. I will crush socialism once and for all. I am successful, I am powerful, I am strong and stable. I will get free trade deals with everyone, within two years, without having to give them anything because I am successful, I am powerful, I am strong and stable.

This is how I imagine Theresa May is thinking, like a motivational speaker talking to the mirror...usually because they know what they're selling is a lie.

Wales' leaders, elected in 2016, never bought the Brexit bus hook, line, and stinker like England's. Immediately after the vote, our First Minister Carwyn Jones said that the vote would be respected but we wouldn't leave the single market because that would kill our economy. It's a very difficult political position for the Welsh government: unlike Northern Ireland and Scotland, Wales voted 52.5%-47.5% to leave the EU. Though that's above the national vote, it's still the second lowest of all the Leave regions and so was a close-cut thing. However, broadcasters like to embellish it for dramatic effect with the words 'Wales voted overwhelmingly to Leave' – it was actually a narrow win. So Carwyn set out six key priorities which led to a White Paper that Welsh Labour and Plaid Cymru published together and recommended staying in the EEA and EFTA, i.e. take the Norway model. Carwyn even took the savvy move of going to Norway in January and did the important 'making close friends' thing.

With Theresa all set for a hard Brexit, this White Paper has been summarily ignored by Westminster. Should Jeremy Corbyn be prime minister when you're reading this, he's already said we'll remain in the EEA and EFTA. Without the single market, we're dead in the water – of course, I would say that as I'm a politically engaged type whereas many in my family and many I grew up with would tell me I don't know what I'm talking about.

Full disclosure: I'm a member of Welsh Labour and I like Carwyn Jones as a politician, as a man, and as someone who has done a lot for Wales. I also respect him because he's bloody tall – a giant in Welsh terms – at six foot something. He doesn't look that imposing on TV but, damn, combined with his history and achievements, he's got stature.

Stature and standing that he has, it has done us in Wales no good in the Brexit process and the divisions between Welsh Labour and UK Labour are all too clear to the politically engaged at general election time. Try as the Welsh government might to remind Westminster that all devolved assemblies are constitutionally required to be consulted, whatever the Supreme Court says, they haven't listened to or involved devolved governments. Remember: nobody but Theresa May's team saw her Article 50 letter before it was sent; the Joint Ministerial Commission was set up to ensure the devolved governments and Westminster all worked together on major issues...but the current UK government has a 'tin ear' – as Carwyn put it – so it is that England forges ahead with its 'Empire 2.0' plans (yes, they're called that and yes, it probably was BoJo's idea). So it is that England doesn't actually listen to Northern Ireland, Scotland, or Wales. This, this is the feeling in Wales. Scotland and – who I feel most sorry for – Northern Ireland, too.

If we look at Carwyn's six points, which have Westminster taken on board?

1. *Protect jobs and economic confidence?* Prices are up, sterling is down, Nestlé factories and most banks are moving to the EU.

2. *Play a full part in discussions on EU withdrawal?* Nope. See 'tin ear'.

3. *Retain access to the European single market?* Hard Brexit says no.

4. *Negotiate continued involvement in major EU funding programmes, such as for farming and poorer areas?* Hard Brexit says NOoooo.

5. *Revise the Treasury's funding formula for the Welsh government budget?* Not a peep out of Westminster.

6. *Put the relationship between devolved administrations and the UK government on an 'entirely different footing'?* London has left Northern Ireland without help, without a government, and easily within reach of the Troubles of old. In a way, it is an entirely different footing – one of aggression.

Want to ask me again why I'm pissed off? No, I didn't think so. In fact, I think you should be too. Many in Wales definitely are. This makes #GE2017 volatile. Volatile things are dangerous – often deadly... I just hope they're not deadly for my side...

April 25th, 2017 — In order to use my anger productively, I'm actively campaigning for an independent Wales with Yes Cymru. We're a group of non-partisan campaigners who, like Scotland, want each nation of the British Isles to be on equal footing. Some people might call me a nationalist, I call myself a rationalist and internationalist.

As you've hopefully seen from this writing alone, the nations aren't on an equal footing – as I write, Westminster are risking lives in Northern Ireland and taking lives up and down the country by their savage, ideologically driven, austerity policies; they aren't listening to or funding the other devolved governments properly, either. When the author of the funding agreement, Lord Barnett, says it was a 'terrible mistake', perhaps it should be changed. You'd think that, if reasonable people were in government, reasonable people would get to changing it. You'd think that, wouldn't you.

Umberto Eco defined 'ur-fascism' in 1995 in *The New York Review of Books* and right now, the UK has 12 of the 14 symptoms he diagnosed; when I first read Eco's piece, I was struck by how much it resembled every move David Cameron was making in 2015. Cameron's aide to the 2005 election, Garvan Walshe, recently admitted that they worked hard to up anti-immigrant feeling and kept at it in every election since. If it looks like shit and it smells like shit...

A recent poll put the Conservatives ahead in Wales (for Members of Parliament, not Assembly Members) for the first time since 1918. Ten points ahead. They're so far ahead likely because a majority of UKIP members have fled to the new home of fascism, the Conservative Party. Theresa and friends are playing by the same book that Cameron did with a whack of the BNP's 2005 manifesto and it may well work.

A massive part of my desire for an independent Wales is to halt the spread of fascism, ableism, sexism, and xenophobia that's crawling from Thanet-on-Sea, ever westward, ever evolving to absorb people's fears and turn them against others.

So, yes, I'm a nationalist now. Not a saluting, frothing nationalist of old but a pragmatic nationalist. A nationalist that just wants what's fair and halts fascism; a nationalist that wants to work with its immediate neighbours, not against; an international nationalist. Notice the small 'n'. Not only am I member of Yes Cymru, I'm also a founding member of Labour for an Independent Wales – encouraging every Welsh Labour member to consider how much better and fairer Wales could be.

Welsh Labour are in power in the Senedd but they can only buffer against England's rising fascism until 2021, when the next Welsh elections are. If the Conservatives continue to dominate, UKIP eats itself, and UK Labour continues to refuse to make a 'progressive alliance', then the recent poll which put Conservatives ahead may seem eerily familiar in the 2021 Welsh Assembly elections too – all in time for *Children of Men* to be a reality in all but the infertility.

After all this electoral doom and gloom, the question you're likely asking now is: why is all this happening? Isn't Wales supposed to 'keep a welcome in the hillside'? Isn't Wales a warm country anymore? Weren't we devastated enough by Thatcher treating us like second class citizens? Didn't the miners' strike teach us to never vote Tory again?

You'd think we'd have memories long enough for the miners' strike at just under 35 years but you have to understand three main things: one, Wales is incredibly poor compared with the rest of the UK; two, we don't have our own media; three, the old are more likely to vote.

Never underestimate what poverty does to you. Poverty is stressful. Poverty will make you forget, in an instant, what's happened before; it will make you stay in abusive situations; it will leave you open to charlatans who promise you the moon on a stick and tell you it's the immigrants' fault you're poor. Poverty makes you blinkered: when you're young, hungry, tired, and quick to boil over, kick off, or steal what you need instead of waiting then you don't see a wide horizon in front of you, only aggressors on each side of you. You don't vote because it's not worth it. Today, a Trussell Trust report showed that 95,190 people in Wales use food banks. In 2016, The Joseph Rowntree Foundation estimated that 23% of Wales' population are in poverty. That's around 700,000 people. That's enough to swing a vote – especially when they're lied to and only see a few sources to go to.

Considering that Theresa May recently stood in Bridgend talking about how 'Wales is an important part of our country' when Wales is *already* a country, not a region; considering BoJo chooses to hark back to the Empire in not just his lack of diplomacy but his very language; it seems clear to me that colonialism and a colonialism of the mind play a large part in Wales' problems too. If you're above 60 in any part of the UK, you're more likely to have been brought up being told the Empire was a great thing. That's a lot of votes going Empire 2.0's way.

When I say 'we don't have our own media' you might balk. 'What about all that Welsh language media our taxes and TV licenses pay for?' you'd balkily balk and you might be half right. There's a bit of Welsh language media out there: BBC Cymru Fyw online, newspapers even, and S4C, but roughly 80% of the country isn't fluent in Welsh. Fi, er enghraifft: dwi darllen Cymraeg ac defnyddio hyn gyda fy deulu ond dwi dal angen i wneud mwy (*Me, for example: I read Welsh and use it with my family but I still need to do more*). Roughly half a million people use Welsh daily but not necessarily enough to have their full, complicated life lived out exclusively in Welsh. Those that do number around 300,000. So for 85%-90% of Wales, that media is discounted; that leaves the local papers, WalesOnline, and...the English press.

Growing up, I rarely saw a newspaper that wasn't *The Sun*, *The Daily Mail*, or the *Shropshire Star*. Shropshire is an English county. *The Daily Mail* and *The Sun* don't exactly broadcast the Welsh government's successes – in fact, they actively disparage them and make culturally racist 'jokes' about the intelligence, the sexuality, and the ability of Welsh people.

'But all that's changing with social media and free online news, right?' Wrong. If you're too poor to afford enough food, you're not buying a smartphone – if your kid wants one and you somehow get one then you're not replacing it if it breaks. Your local library gets shut down so you and yours can't use the computers there; when it costs too much to go to the one a town over, you just stop going.

The only news you then see is the TV or the newsstand. Both BBC Wales News and ITV Cymru News are preceded by UK news, meaning a lot of people turn off at that point (missing a national treasure, Derek The Weather). To illustrate this, annual surveys ask people what they want for and how much they know about the Senedd – this year, 30% of people thought Westminster runs the NHS in Wales. This 30% are misinformed: Wales is the only government in the UK to not have cut its NHS funding. NHS Wales isn't privatised either. This illustrates the definite need for an English language newspaper – like Scotland's *The National* – to get relevant news, culture, history, and a sense of our place in the world to Wales.

I've talked about free movement a bit here. Talked about Portugal some too – it may not be obvious why. Did you know Portugal and the UK are the oldest recorded allies in the world? It was ratified by the Anglo-Portuguese Treaty of 1373. About 90 years after England had conquered Wales. England would likely have conquered Portugal if it could. Portugal had a huge navy.

Portugal is now, like many places, divided by north and south: in the north, people have the same income as those in Wales; in the south, people have the same income as those in England (outside London). In the 21st century, Portugal and Wales have a lot in common. Portugal just has a lot more sun. They are an economically divided people but through the EU, they get by pretty well. Food here is cheap, wine is just as cheap, and they make the best use of their biggest natural resources: the wind and the sun. Wales' history is of a European country, Wales' future could be too. Regarding natural resources: Wales is paid nothing for the water it provides to Birmingham but a London registered company is – when that figure is £263 million per year (at £0.002p/litre), you can begin to understand how we might get by too. Especially when we provide Liverpool as well.

There are so many other European countries similar to Wales. Take Croatia: twice the size but has less economic output. Take the 17 other independent countries in the European Union *smaller* than Wales. Let's ask, did they have everything they needed to make a country before they were a fully formed nation? No. Does Wales? Yup. Devolution has given us plenty of wheels of government. We're very happy to use them.

All of those wheels wouldn't have been built without the EU. The laws used to create the Senedd in the first place come directly from Europe. Same for Holyrood and Stormont. Even though some may not know everything our Senedd does, 50% of the country agree that it should have more powers while the other 50% are divided or don't know.

Much like Portugal is split in the middle, Wales is too: the west voted to Remain, the east to Leave. There are plenty of hill farmers in the west and they know their Common Agricultural Payments from the EU are absolutely necessary to small farm survival but so too are the hard fought for, EU-backed environmental protections that ensure traditional methods for flood prevention have been brought back (because they actually work, unlike dredging). In the east, there are plenty of lowland farmers who've bought the lie that they'd receive just as much funding from London as the EU. If we do leave, they'll feel the drop first. All of this is just a fraction of the reasoning for Wales to be independent and in the EU. Also: wine. And neighbourliness. And adventure.

At 32, I'm not so young nor so old as to group myself anywhere outside 'people in their 30s' but considering that the majority of people below 40 voted to remain in the EU, let's hope they can make their voice heard at #GE2017. Let's hope they keep us in the EU so they can have adventures like mine.

The Wales I want to see is outward looking; Wales could be green and red – environmental and industrial; a small nation arm-in-arm with other small nations. It's worth repeating: without the single market, we're dead in the water. If Wales goes blue and hard Brexit ensues, we might as well be the water.

I want Welsh Labour to lead the case for independence – if they don't get out ahead of the political headwind that's coming if/when the economy crashes, they'll be swept away by a tide of Plaid Cymru as Scottish Labour were by the SNP.

There's an economic case, a democratic (deficit) case, and an emotional case to be made for Welsh independence. Name me a problem you think we'll face, I'll have an answer. For too long we've been told we're too poor, too small, or too stupid – well welcome to the 21st century, bud, where the British Foreign Secretary is stupid and the two smartest, savviest politicians in British politics are the leaders of the Welsh and the Scottish Assemblies.

So now you know Wales, what does all this tell us about the upcoming election? It tells us that the left wing of politics has a bigger fight on its hands than ever before. Welsh Labour continue to support its MP candidates and Plaid Cymru, with its record of being the hardest working MPs in Westminster, may make some gains. Let's hope UKIP have been seen for the phonies they are and the 2021 elections will see them kicked out of the Senedd too.

It's likely that that recent poll giving the Tories a 10-point lead will fade and things will balance out at about 30/30 – of course, I'd like it not to. I'd like the Tories to get the fuck out of Wales and know of two Welsh Tory MPs that might be under investigation in the election expenses fraud cases that might just be forced to fail. If I'm too honest, that poll made me concerned; so concerned that I booked myself into an event titled 'Spring Dinner with the First Minister'.

April 28th, 2017 — As we sat down at our table, we were greeted warmly by those sat near us and quick introductions were made in Welsh and English – it immediately felt like a truly bilingual event with the welcoming of experienced and inexperienced speakers alike. This welcoming is what I want for Wales. This welcoming is what I know Wales to be.

The average age at the table before we joined couldn't have dropped below 65. The fact that my date was below 40 and one of only two people of colour at the event was bad. We need a lot more diversity and young people in politics. Carwyn even said so later.

Politically, the room was plenty diverse. I don't know if I've ever been sat so close to people who own two houses before. The very first question put to Carwyn after his – funny, measured, sensible – speech was from my table-mate and about exactly that; Carwyn somehow managed the difficult task of smoothing it out while answering frankly.

This is representative of his approach to the coming #GE2017. As we were sworn to Chatham House rules, I can't quote much of what was said but much of it was the UK Labour party line...but with a feeling that the Welsh government are rattling at their chains. Nowhere near as radical as I'd wanted but a hint of a hope of a flint of fight.

He chose to mention his sensible approach of forging coalition governments in the Senedd (which, without even saying so, highlights a disappointment with UK Labour for not doing so) but still toed the party line when asked about his hopes for federalism in the UK, going only so far as to say that seeing as how Canada has it 'it's not radical'. He called for grown-up politics, intelligent and passionate politics, one removed from insults and one with more diverse politicians.

In the Senedd, Carwyn is one of two leaders who aren't clowns or untrustworthy. The leader of the Welsh Conservatives, Andrew RT Davies, is – well let me just say never have I seen a man who so embodies the term Dic Siôn Dafydd (before 'Uncle Tom' or 'quisling', there was Dic Sion Dafydd). Davies recently welcomed a UKIP AM into their ranks, Mark Reckless. Reckless has form on this: he jumped from Tories to UKIP just last year. UKIP leader is Neil Hamilton, he of the Cash for Questions scandal – he is, like Nigel Farage, in it for the money and power, nothing more; it's obvious to anyone that looks at his record that he doesn't care for Wales. He doesn't even live in Wales. UKIP recently announced that Wales needed to stay in EEA and EFTA, too – the very party that exists to take us out! Reckless by name... Such is the colonial mentality that voters would accept this from our politicians. The Lib Dems have proven to be allies to this Senedd but who knows which way they'll blow should a Tory-led Welsh government come to pass. Leanne Wood is the other elected AM and leader who is obviously human and capable; she played sharp politics last year when the Senedd looked to be hung, the Tories were sniffing for power, and UKIP looked like possible kingmakers; she played a lot of people off of each other but she also played with fire when working with UKIP. Carwyn didn't swing to the hard right like that; Welsh Labour had the fortune of being the largest party with just one more AM needed on their side.

Carwyn is a rock. A giant. The simple truth is, he's ground at by the mechanisms of an outdated constitution. My date, who knew very little of Welsh politics before, later described him as 'very human, very warm but firm, intelligent, and so unlike English politicians – like a tree' and so he stands. A giant rooted in party history. He said that if constitutionally and economically threatened, the Welsh government would 'resist'. Many in Wales don't believe him because of his professional, never insulting manner. Though I know I'm more radical than him and must admit to being disappointed by his choice to toe the party line, any resistance against fascism with him in it is a resistance that I'd be a part of. I don't know if he has the fire to lead it but I do know he has the good sense to guide and to build it.

Questions were taken after his speech. They were many and varied; I waited to see if the 'I' word, independence, would raise its head. It didn't, only federalism; the party line again. Yet hadn't his speech spoken of resisting?

I detect in Carwyn a man who wants to work with what we've got but knows it's woefully unfair; a man who wants to break free from the shackles of both party and the status quo but cannot bring himself to upturn the table – perhaps because he knows he can protect Wales for four more years. Perhaps he's biding his time, perhaps not. He hides his light under a bushel well when in a room of lawyers and likely Conservative voters.

What I've written feels more like bringing you up to speed, not a prediction. Like I'm helping you understand the frustrations, the systematic inequalities, and the curiosities of Wales. I can only hope that it's fair on you and fairer still on my fellow Cymraeg.

It's not unfair to say we've long fought for our survival and the survival of the spirit of Wales. In 2017, the fight is starting all over again. Good thing we're a hardy, scrappy, smart bunch. We can only hope that, as the leader of the Welsh people, Carwyn Jones ensures our survival – with or without England – when the time comes.

Ben Gwalchmai is a maker, worker, writer who was WNO's writer-in-residence, a Historical Novel Society 'Editor's Pick' for his novel Purefinder*, and is undertaking a PhD at NUI, Galway. He grew up in Powys, Wales, and still regularly works on farms and in pubs there.*

SCOTLAND: THE DAYS OF THE 56

by Peter Burnett

In 2015, Scotland sent 56 out of 59 MPs to Westminster, whose goal was Scottish independence. Nicola Sturgeon stood for election as First Minister of Scotland in 2016 on a mandate to seek a second referendum on independence, and the majority of the Scots voted in an SNP government on that understanding. We know that the days of the 56 MPs in Westminster may be over in June 2017, yet theirs is a landmark achievement. Mhairi Black is one of the principals of the 56 and the passion of her maiden speech explains why so many support the SNP.

In the speech, Mhairi Black tells the story of a man who fainted on a bus, and was 15 minutes late for a jobseeker's appointment and consequently sanctioned for thirteen weeks. She says:

> When the Chancellor spoke in his budget about fixing the roof while the sun is shining, I have to ask: on whom is the sun shining? When he spoke about benefits not supporting certain kinds of lifestyles, is that the kind of lifestyle he was talking about? And when the Minister for Employment was asked to consider if there was a correlation between the number of sanctions and the rise in food bank use, she stated: 'Food banks play an important role in local welfare

provision.' (But) food banks are NOT a part of the welfare state, they are a symbol that the welfare state is failing.

Mhairi Black concluded by addressing the Labour benches, saying that like so many others she comes from a traditional socialist working class family, and she is confident when she says that: 'It is the Labour Party that left me, not the other way about.'

In England, the snap general election of 2017 will be cast as a Tories versus Labour rout. Or something like that. However, we in Scotland will likely be watching those two parties scrambling for crumbs again, while we work on our decision as to how many of our 56 we wish to return, or in fact if we want to return more. I just read George Monbiot's recent findings on 'what the Jocks are up to', summed up in the subheading: 'Whenever I visit Scotland, I'm reminded that Britain is politically dead from the neck down.'

I discover the same thing when I visit England, where politics is not any less discussed, but instead is more whispered. Here in Scotland, Monbiot's right, we're charged with it like electricity, and since the referendum of 2014, popular activity has begun to overtake hot air in some areas. We have more happening on the ground than is ever reported, even by our political blogs, and I am referring to what are known as social movements – people activating and doing things in different ways. Why is this politics? It's because doing things such as starting businesses with social aims, counts as doing the government's work for them – and volunteers and businesses do the government's work for them all the time in Scotland, and many of us would like to do more.

The first thing is that we are allowed to do the government's work in Scotland. It's like our right to roam – it's just unthinkable that there are places we can't go. One example that typifies a few of these surprise grassroots moves is the Peoples' Council, which forms small councils which hold their local councils accountable, and through them try and make change. Their motto is brilliant: Act as if you own the place. I like the motto because, co-incidentally, we do own the place. In April 2017, the People's Council created a hustings event with a focus on participation from the public including voting on key issues. This idea and other conceptions like it work because face to face meetings between people and representatives make the councils accountable.

The People's Council, formed in 2015, writes:

> Local democracy has long been the victim of centralisation; of national government 'trimming the fat' of local authorities in order to make efficiency savings. Now, when many of our politicians talk of the need for more local democracy, what they are really talking about is 'devolving the axe' – more trimming of the state, this time by making communities responsible for cuts, and using volunteers to plug gaps left in the system.

This foundational group has produced research, manifestos and reports promoting the far less glamorous business of local government, and they have done it well. The late Paddy Bort said at their first 2015 meeting that in Norway he was seeing populations between 3,000 – 20,000 per council region compared to 170,000 in Scotland. One of the best things about the People's Council is that it is also based outside of Edinburgh, which tells more about the deep personal and social leanings of the Scots.

In Scotland, we have been telling the rest of the world for ages that some of this isn't even about independence – we've been telling you it's about hope and change – our hope that we can change things, and being allowed to do that.

What we like about our Parliament is that it's manageable, we like the size, we like the fact that we can touch our politicians, and we like that they are among us. Those living in Edinburgh have most of them at one time run into Nicola Sturgeon somewhere, in Charlotte Square, with some of her friends, or at an event. Is that not in fact utopian?

I don't need to remind anyone in Scotland that England is a separate country, but this can sometimes surprise others. The thing about Scotland's independence is that it needs to be seen from our point of view to work, so sorry England, and sorry Monbiot. When Theresa May says 'politics is not a game,' she reveals that politics is in fact a game. The game has rules such as: 'Whatever you say about

Britain's relationship with Europe, say the opposite about Scotland's relationship with Britain'. As in a game, Theresa May plays the timing to the best of her advantage, with the aim being the strategic reduction of the 56, and with Ruth Davidson as her number one weapon. The object of the game is to reduce her opposition, and in Westminster, Labour is not Theresa May's opposition. It is the SNP.

Despite making up a weighty percentage of the Westminster opposition, you might hear very little about the 56. You probably hear more about the one UK Independence Party seat. But the 56 are there and I will be approaching the 2017 snap election in celebrating their individual success and their collective achievement: good government in Scotland and good government in England.

And we are a poetic nation as well you are aware. We have couplets for them all – and if you don't believe me let's meet some at random:

GAVIN NEWLANDS MP
Gavin Newlands plays for Paisley Rugby Club
At 12 joined the party's youth wing
Overturned a Labour majority
With a 27% swing.

PATRICIA GIBSON MP
Patricia Gibson from Kilburnie
Proved Labour promises barren
Is married to an SNP MSP
And is MP for N. Ayrshire and Arran.

JOHN NICHOLSON MP
One of National Collective
On television's ten best-dressed list
Tabled the Alan Turing Law
After coming out on BBC Breakfast.

ANGUS MACNEIL MP
Angus MacNeil has been an MP
Since 2005.
Once kissed and fondled two lovers
For which he's since apologised.

MARTYN DAY MP
For a vision
His ambition
The abolition
Of the Lords
In Britain.

JOHN MCNALLY MP
John McNally was a barber from Denny
In Falkirk the people's choice.
Won more votes than any candidate's ever won
And knocked out Eric Joyce.

DEIRDRE BROCK MP
Leith loves that Deirdre
Cleared the
Labour party away fae
Ward and Seat!

DOUGLAS CHAPMAN MP

Used to be a councillor in Rosyth
Where they built the submarines he's
Now gonnae fight.

MARTIN DOCHERTY MP

Fought poverty for a decade in West Dunbarton-
shire Community and Voluntary Services.
Became the cause of Gemma Doyle MP's
Electoral nervousness.

CALUM KEIR MP

Lo, Kerr thy upward countenance stares
Wise on the portfolio of Rural Affairs!
Still man, way to go.
You did it in a constituency that voted two thirds
to one third NO.

EILIDH WHITEFORD MP

Making poverty history
Is worth pursuing,
Though Ian Davidson's
Threatening a doing.

CORRI WILSON MP

No matter what the defence is
Family members paid from parliamentary
expenses
Will always have its consequences.

These are twelve heroic examples and we will have poems and songs for them all in time, you can be sure of that. Yet today we are curious to see how many will remain in Westminster because we fear it may never be topped. This would be a pity because the prize of a second referendum is so very near and we will need every one of them there to ensure it comes in time.

And so it is with apologies to the other nations voting, that I inform you that this is what the 2017 election is about. Meantime and for historical records, the two members of the 56 who are not coming back in 2017 are both barred. These are Michelle Thomson, a former SNP MP now sitting as an independent, who has been disqualified from standing due to an unresolved legal case. Another former SNP MP, Natalie McGarry, has also been barred from standing again for the party in Glasgow East after being charged with fraud. She has also been sitting as an independent in the Commons.

The days of the 56 commenced on the 7th May 2015, and since then and throughout Brexit, I have referred countless people to the map of the British Isles with its entirely yellow Scotland. 'Does that or does that not look like a separate country?' I ask. The SNP won all but three of Scotland's 59 Westminster seats in 2015. All of the other sitting 54 have been reselected automatically. Remain is also always pictured as yellow, of course.

Scotland always has been an independent

country, and I was surprised when I grew up to hear that it was not. Different political parties have run that country, usually Labour, and in the 1980s and 1990s the SNP were a fringe party, lower in status and popularity than any. There isn't a lot of difference between the way that the Labour Party ran the country then and the way the SNP run the country now, but Labour have broken down so grievously in Scotland, they don't even deserve another chance. Individual Labour candidates may be suitable for representation in 2017, but what is the point when the leaders are so confused/confusing?

So instead of Labour, we now have the 56, and I am amazed to say that I live in a country in which 95% of the electoral seats are held by one single party! Ordinarily that would sound awful, but it's not. I live in a democracy, enviable in the western world as it contains no visible far right. Immigration and refugees in particular continue to be welcomed. We have more social enterprise going on here, and short of gaining the remaining three Scottish seats in Westminster, there is nothing left for it but for the SNP to start fielding candidates in England. Their representatives work well in Westminster, at least as well as the Labour MPs did in Westminster when they had 50 or more so seats that they don't have any more. And what is wrong with a centre-left, socially-guided political party? I don't think England have even got one.

What England have instead I find out is a warped dystopian version of the SNP in a party called the English Democrats, who live in a separatist England, and seek to devolve England from the 1707 Union. The English Democrats argue that they are 'neither left nor right, just English' but from their manifesto, and the concerns flagged up on the homepage of their website, I would assess their politics as veering severely to the starboard.

I ask myself, why would the Scottish separatist party be a left-leaning organisation and the English equivalent be so obviously to the right? England is heaving with right wing parties, they cannot get enough of them. They have the BNP and the British Democratic Party as well as the Britannic Party and a thing called the British Unity Party (now featuring Nick Griffin) – then there is Liberty GB, Britain First and of course there's UKIP – and all of these are available to you when the Conservatives just aren't right wing enough.

In Scotland we don't have any of these guys. The worst we can say is that we have a disintegrated far left, which has failed to function in recent years almost as well as the Labour party has failed to function.

Eyes on the prize however – the second referendum. As we near June 2017 economic arguments will commence fast and furious and the scaremongering will begin. It will be long-view scaremongering, scaremongering not just into the winter of 2017, but scaremongering for a long cold future few years hence, when Scotland will be independent.

This is a shame because economic arguments are notoriously changeable and based on remote facts and speculations, and all of this can serve many simultaneous and contradictory ends. But you know that already! This is why I as a voting Scot have always gone for the clarity of a sound emotive argument, and been obliged to ridicule facts. The oil price doesn't affect my thoughts on Scotland's future, either, even though you think it should.

The only thing, to be honest that effects my thoughts on Scotland's future is the Conservative Party, and it is not just because they have had such a ruinous effect on its past. Most everybody who has said anything about Scotland's Tories' chances in the 2017 election have at one point used the phrase 'resurgent Tories.' You can hear the word 'resurgent' or varieties of it used in conjunction with 'Tories' on the nation's news and you just know the reporters are being told to say it. It's the same way that different newsrooms mysteriously started calling Edward Snowden a 'fame-seeking narcissist' for a short while there in 2013. They don't exactly send a memo round but these guys just pick up on each other.

Part of this magic is down to the seeming popularity of Ruth Davidson, a woman who, like Margaret Thatcher, looks good in a tank. In truth nothing matters about Ruth Davidson, tanks or her other forms of motorised transport, which I'll come to. Ruth Davidson remains a Tory, and that is a problem in this country. You might have heard the phrase 'Tartan Tories', which was coined by Labour to put down the SNP. As a debating tactic, it is poor, as the two have little in common. But I mention it because it tells more about the Tories than it does about the SNP. It tells you that the worst, the grossest insult you can make to someone in Scotland, is to call them a Tory.

This is because people are dying in Scotland and it is due to Tory policy. It goes back a long way now and although the Tories can pretend to ignore the SNP in Westminster, they cannot in Scotland, where the parliamentary makeup is different.

The resurgence of the Tories is therefore an optical illusion. There is no doubt that the SNP will do well in 2017's UK general election but it is likely to lose a few of its massive 56 seats. These are seats which will go the Tories, who have a chance to seek out and woo the few pockets of pro-Brexit individuals in Scotland, and grab a vote. It's not a resurgence, but it is radical. It is so wild that the Labour Party are losing votes to the Tories, a quite unthinkable thing under typical conditions.

If you are not in Scotland, you will have missed the dumbfounding now daily Tory election leaflets which prove all of this. Wingsoverscotland.com ('the less-deserving pro-independence website') has been collecting and publishing these, and the chief curiosity among them is that while the SNP have ceased talking about independence and have concentrated on policy – the Tories have revealed a single-message campaign, warning of the perils of independence and wisely (in their case) ignoring policy.

The reason the Tories can behave like this in Scotland – the neck-up part of the UK – is their belief that the charm of Ruth Davidson is sufficient to win seats. Ruth is someone you could go for a pint with. Ruth cracks a braw smile – including in a recent exploit in which she rode an all-terrain mobility vehicle and was photographed grinning like a white-socked lottery winner while doing so. The underlying message as with the Tories in Scotland was exceedingly stark. Earlier in the same month the charity Motability, which manages mobility vehicles for disabled people, released figures that 51,000 people had seen their vehicles removed as a result of Tory policy since 2013. It's the distinct flavour of Toryism in Scotland, overt and for those that can see it, cynical.

One popular 2017 election leaflet has a message from Ruth Davidson, ending: '[the SNP] should be improving our economy. You have my guarantee the Scottish Conservatives will oppose them every step of the way.'

There are hundreds of active separatist movements and parties across Europe, and each has a story. Scotland may seem like it's always been trouble for England, one way or another, but voting for independence is pretty new to us. The SNP existed as a curiosity since its beginnings in the 1928 National Party of Scotland, founded by among others, the dissident bard Hugh MacDiarmid. But nobody very much voted for the SNP for seventy years, until Scotland got its own parliament. That alone has always told me that we seek independence. It was the fact that when we saw the parliament, it really became obvious we had to fill it with our own politics. For these reasons I take Canarian nationalism, Basque independence, Andalusian nationalism, Hungarian regional autonomy for Serbs, Sardinian nationalism, and the nationalism of Lombardians, Frisians, Normands, Bretons and others, all seriously.

The best argument that I've seen for Scottish independence lately was expressed in Michael Moore's film *Where To Invade Next* (2015). The film doesn't mention Scotland, but in the picture, Moore tours lesser and roughly left-leaning European states, many of which would be smaller or equivalent in size and economy to an independent Scotland. In each state, Michael Moore looks at one social service, the big idea being that he's invading these countries and taking their good stuff back to America. Scotland would have really fitted into this movie if it was independent, although what we would offer cannot be seen, although I am sure we would begin experimenting straight away.

Michael Moore looked at the following however:

• In Italy, he looked at labour rights and workers' wellbeing

• In France, he looked at school meals and sex education

- In Finland, he considered education policy and spoke to the Finnish Minister of Education

- In Slovenia, he looked at debt-free higher education

- In Germany he discovered the work-life balance of the population, and considered the values of honest, frank national history education

- In Portugal, he looked at drug policy

- In Norway, he looked at their humane prison system

- In Tunisia, he was told about women's rights, including reproductive health, access to abortion and their role in the Tunisian Revolution and the drafting of the Tunisian Constitution of 2014

- In Iceland he looked at women in power, speaking with Vigdís Finnbogadóttir, the world's first democratically elected female president. He also looked at the 2008–11 Icelandic financial crisis and the criminal investigation and prosecution of bankers, with special prosecutor Ólafur Hauksson.

Once again, this is the prize. The prize for any vote in the UK in 2017, is to let Scotland be free of a Westminster parliament which obliges pomp, inefficiency, and outright conservatism – oh and conservatism too. Other things that we don't like or need would include unaccountable politics, which are a poison to Scotland, even if the Tories think they could work for England. The prize in this election for Scotland is the chance to be a government like one of the above – to be a state that can take steps to build a government fitting the needs of its immediate constituents.

I agree with Mhairi Black when she says that the SNP did not triumph on a wave of nationalism, but on a wave of hope that representatives like herself could give a voice to those who didn't have one, the implication being that the Labour Party had given up listening to Scotland after delivering the Scottish Parliament in 1999. This – the most important part of Mhairi Black's maiden speech was addressed to the Labour Party – not the Tories. In it she urged them to join her in forming an effective opposition to the government.

'We must oppose, not abstain,' she said to Labour. That is Scottish fighting talk for 'Down with the Tories.'

With thanks to Lynzi Leroy

Peter Burnett is a writer and publisher based in Edinburgh. He is a director at The Scottish Design Exchange and for his third day job, he runs Scotland's first Virtual Reality Arcade E-VR.

'PAISLEY SAID YES': REFLECTIONS ON NEW DIVIDING LINES IN UK POLITICS

by Richard Price

'Scots are not genetically designed to make political decisions.' – Johann Lamont, the then Leader of the Labour Party in Scotland, 2014

JP O'Malley: So you see the distinctions in terms of class – throughout Britain – rather than a big difference in culture?
John Burnside: In a very sort of old left way, I find the whole Scottish nationalist issue an irritation. We are all expected to vote on whether we are going to be independent or not, and the undercurrent of that is an idea that we will somehow be free. Right now a vote for the referendum on the Scottish independence issue would be taken as an endorsement of Scottish nationalism, and that is not the issue. We should be working together, rather than concentrating on this national borderline question. That just takes away from the real questions: such as poverty, equality, and social justice.
Interview with John Burnside, *The Bottle Imp*, Spring 2014

On Thursday 18th September 2014 Scotland went to the polling booths to answer the question 'Should Scotland be an independent country?' In answering that question, Scotland became perhaps the first country in history to win itself a referendum on self-determination only to lose its sovereignty in the vote: 55% said 'No.'

Whatever your views, that is surely a world record no country can be proud of, but then which 'country' are we talking about? Does this result suggest that Scotland is only a country in certain senses, while the UK can be proud, the theory would go, that it can air such questions within its democratic apparatus and that in fact, to do so, would seem to show that it is the UK that is the country, while Scotland has moved further towards regionalising itself? Lukewarm acknowledgement of statehood at a referendum is no way to assert independence.

Two years later, in a spectacularly misjudged effort to appease the Eurosceptics in his party and the growing force of UKIP, David Cameron took the UK into another referendum and this time one country did, just, assert what it saw as its independence: England. 53.4% of English voters voted to leave the European Union, enough of a percentage to carry the other nations and territories with it, even though Scotland voted 62% to remain. It's fascinating, though also chilling, to find that what were in fact both very marginal referendums have solidified into political phrases such as 'the nation has clearly spoken' when the best that can be said is that there is a welter of different opinions forced into the

binary choice: profound disagreement, perhaps a little disagreement (but enough to vote another way),
or even ambivalence, certainly mixed feelings. One
thing is clear: the nation – whatever nation we are
talking about – has not clearly spoken. It has mum-
bled, it has argued aloud to itself, answering shout
with shout, whisper with whisper; it is a mess of in-
coherence. Only opportunists would pretend there
has been certainty in these votes, and so it is the opportunists – the Conservatives – who have so readily traduced these referendums' complex meanings.

After the Scottish referendum was the time to have
one of those boring but utterly essential discussions about whether in a referendum of such far
reaching consequences a simple majority should
really hold sway. Would Yes really have relished
independence on the back of the kind of vote that
Leave got in the European Referendum? Some,
perhaps, but that is no way to make such a change.
    Even to talk this way, however, is to hybrid-
ise two very different kinds of emotional response:
it is to talk constitutionally (in tonal terms, 'dry')
and nationalistically (in tonal terms, 'dry') and even
nationalistically (in tonal terms, 'hot-headed') –
though 'nationalism' is a much more tricky concept
than John Burnside perhaps had to space to discuss,
a topic I'll return to later. When one talks constitutionally, even using the harder, apparently purer
word, 'sovereignty', where are the issues of 'poverty, equality, and social justice' which John Burnside

rightly identifies as so pressing? They could get forgotten if you weren't careful.

As a long-term resident of London, having left Scotland in 1988, I am both the wrong and right person to ask about these issues. From my royal armchair somewhere in North London I supported and encouraged the Yes Movement in Scotland. I was probably childishly proud that the town nearest to where I grew up, Paisley, voted Yes and I still believe that Scotland should be an independent country. I understand the argument about it seldom 'being the time' to talk about or act to change different government systems, never mind create new states from old ones (because the existing frameworks have too much on their plate, dealing with everyday issues, etcetera).

Really, that is an argument about short term pragmatism always obliterating long term strategic thinking. Long term is anathema to the political system because of limited political terms, the fake urgency of the shrill news agenda, and because strategic change requires investment that does not give a return quickly: put simply the idea of working for a better future is a nightmare for politicians. Most people, especially those who are locked into the effects of deeply-rooted bad political and industrial management, which is the history in the UK of the last forty or so years, are also conditioned to see societal strategic thinking as 'merely' constitutional or to do with governance, without valuing what that might mean to them and to future generations.

Yet, the Scottish referendum on the Yes side never felt like an experiment in political philosophy. At no time was there a feeling that the debate was about constitutional niceties, about the tidiness of proper borders, or that sort of thing. The Better Together campaign fixated on those, and even Ed Miliband, an otherwise pretty sensible politician, emphasised there would be soldiers again at Hadrian's Wall. In the dark hours after the result I am sure I was not alone in wondering if there wasn't a grain of truth in Johann Lamont's quote about Scots being intrinsically unable to make political decisions.

Well, everyone is allowed a temporary low after a vote like that and after a moment of near-despair I, like many other supporters of the Yes movement, and I believe, many who voted No, began to shake that vote and ridiculous quote off. After all, that the Leader of the Labour Party in Scotland should say such a thing said more about that Party's regard for Scots than anything else. Like a hectoring partner in a poisonous relationship, the position of the Labour Party in those days was that Scotland had to be kept under the impression it was a charity case ('gaslighting' is the now-well known term for this), regarded as not quite the shilling mentally (*personifying* an otherwise heterogeneous population is important to rhetorical tactics like this), and with the threat that it would be out on the chilly street without a penny to its name if that relationship broke down. That England's northern partner was in fact educationally advanced, with a developed sense of politics as a working tool for everyday life (not merely for public schoolboy Parliamentary politics), was to be suppressed. If that strategy of threat and belittlement failed, it was to be ridiculed, and if *that* failed, patronised with lip service to the qualities of the country. That Scotland had lately become more than self-sufficient in renewable energy and a highly industrious society was not to be countenanced. Lamont was able to say that because the context is that Scotland is in fact a cash cow for the Union, through oil, through taxes, and, at that time, through taken-for-granted Labour votes (propping up a centre-right consensus in Westminster), so active political decisions were best kept away from them.

As one who supported the Yes movement, I still find it very hard to imagine going into the polling booth and choosing the tired, elitist United Kingdom as a ruling force over the promise of a new country. Moreso because the example of a new Scotland would surely have galvanised the body politic in the remains of the UK. In a way, I guess it did, but with a very dark turn.

    I liken Scotland's role in the Union as being at the back of a tandem – the man at the front (despite notable examples, it almost always is a man) is veering all over the road, shouting, and kicking out at any other road user in the way. At the back, Scotland is a much smaller person (you see, I am going to use this rhetorical tack, too) and can't really see where it's going and doesn't have a choice anyway.

It's always being criticised for just being a passenger but somehow it's doing more than its fair share of the pedalling. When you suggest anything, you're told to pipe down at the back, stop being a back-seat driver. I would have thought anyone would rather get off and walk quietly alone. Maybe it will be slower, but walking surely has more dignity than a tandem bicycle. But I have to admit 55% did say No. They prefer that tandem, their place on that uncomfortable seat at the back. How do we explain that?

I think the first thing to say is that when understanding political votes we are so used to the UK elections' filter, which uses the first past the post system to gauge impact. This was initially reported as a 'game over' situation (it's a similar sleight of hand which berates trades union votes carried on majorities which most MPs would envy – different methods of voting are confusing but that doesn't mean the usual channels should give up on explaining how each works). The BBC News called the 55 / 45 split a 'decisive' vote and the Unionist parties went further, calling it the 'settled will of the Scottish people'. Both these power groupings (since the BBC is, among other things, a power grouping) changed tune subsequently, but I had to gasp at their stretching of language. To use the same ratio at a more imaginable scale: If there are twenty people in a room and nine say one thing and eleven say the opposite, the group may agree to go along with the eleven for the time being but no neutral observer would say a decisive result had been achieved or there was, miraculously, the single settled will of the people in that room. Such an articulation could only be taken as a kind of malign sentimentality, a wish fulfilment of secret or unexamined intent. And it would, by the way, be the same the other way round – if Yes had just inched ahead.

The end result was, though, indicative of the whole referendum process. Instead of answering a single question, the referendum actually brought out into the open many questions, some of them suppressed for years by the nature of the Union itself, including deep class divisions in Scotland (these tend to be romanticised out, because 'everyone's working class in Scotland, aren't they?'). It turned out that those who said No tended to fall into three categories. The first were the well-off and, frankly, the rich. The second were the (largely well-to-do) pensioners who have been protected by the UK parties for years, not because they should be (and they should) but because the parties know a targetable, sizeable and regularly voting cohort when they see one. The final category tended to be traditional Labour voters, especially the more well-off ones. Critically though, a great number of Labour voters had decided that independence was precisely the way to deliver beneficial change as far as poverty, equality, and social justice were concerned: they leapt over the dry constitutional hurdle and embraced the idea that that this was a progressive vote. This is where the loose use of the word 'nationalist' doesn't really work, because it denies the progressive nature, roughly speaking, of the centre-left Scottish National Party, and it sidelines the Scottish Green Party and the Scottish Socialist Party, key players within the Yes movement. Perhaps worst of all, it passively hopes that a socially just transformation of society will be brought about by Westminster and the Labour Party, a demonstrably centrist party for at least the last thirty years. This is why the Scottish referendum was far more than a 'local problem': it called Westminster's bluff, and the Labour Party's bluff, as far as its professed social mission was concerned. And it began to look at the English sytems of power which kept Westminster the way it was.

Such questions were already surfacing months before the vote, in a way that made the Yes movement more like a Scottish Wikileaks at times. For example, did anyone know that the BBC, year after year interviewing spokespeople from The Confederation of British Industry, was actually a paid up member of the CBI itself? We wouldn't know that unless the referendum had happened. To this day, when a CBI mouthpiece pops up on the BBC, the BBC doesn't say, 'now, as you know the BBC belongs to your group, but just for the fun of it pretend we are having an objective conversation about the state of the economy and tell us your views.' They probably don't even see what's wrong. Like the old left in Scotland before the referendum, the old right continues to be naturalised in England: it is just seen as the norm, and as extreme to challenge it. That the spokespeople from the CBI and the Institute of Directors appear many more times to discuss 'the economy' than say, leaders of trade unions who, objectively speaking, have a pretty firm idea of what's happening, too (even experts from finance sector trade unions seldom appear) is another illustration of this personality cult which is internalised and naturalised across the media.

The BBC and the private-funded newspaper press, as so often, were as one on what the referendum was actually about, 'nationalism', and yet 'nationalism' was an unexamined word. I was appalled at the lack of even-handedness and I suppose the poet in me flinched at the sly language they used (micro-tonal inferences are often the way that bias is mobilised, as much perhaps, as structural biases such as the wildly disproportionate publicity the BBC give to the unelected UKIP). Seldom heard were the positives of 'independence' or 'self-determination', but rather the words 'separatism' and 'nationalism' were preferred. The No camp's public obsession with borders and ethnicity got far more than its fair share of media attention. One study of the referendum has shown how the media personalised the referendum – repeating First Minister Alex Salmond's name again and again as if this was a mere general election rather than the rebirth of a country. His name, of course, was not on the ballot, and a country, once free, can vote for whosoever it pleases: again, this presages what has been happening in current times, with Theresa May's language always personalising the general election of 2017 because she knows that Jeremy Corbyn until now has not polled well as a name. The Conservatives are not anti-monarchists, do not believe in a presidential republic, but when it suits them they will act as if they do. The same study of the tactics used by mainstream media in the Scottish referendum shows that for every newspaper article that showed the positives of independence there were more than three that played up potential negatives; worse, for every headline that was positive, there were four headlines that were negative. Of the tens and tens of local and national newspapers only one (Sunday) paper declared for Yes. To use the 'folk in a room' analogy again, the *Sunday Herald* was a lone, quiet voice, in a very crowded room of very shrill shouters, and that room was nothing like faithfully representative of the views of Scottish voters, who, remember, in the end were split almost 50/50 on the idea.

Considering how close the result was, that is a shocking exposure of the reactionary forces in our media, and a tribute to the power of the Yes message even so: from a standing start of just over 20%, Yes did incredibly well. Yes was deliberately not about Scottish ethnicity – there were Poles for Indy and English for Indy groups under the Yes umbrella, for example, welcoming and constructively problematising the idea of the ethnic. Instead, Yes was interested in and inspired by the birth of a modern democracy – it fought on exactly the social justice ticket that the conventional left in Scotland seemed to have abandoned years ago (perhaps hoping the UK 'together' would do something sometime... never). But a modern democracy, if we hadn't known it already, we now know is something many *fear:* especially the disproportionately wealthy, especially big business, especially the big British political parties, (before Jeremy Corbyn's triumph as Labour leader) and especially those right across the media.

This is where it becomes more firmly obvious that the Scottish referendum was only one of several large waves of righteous energy breaking onto the UK as a political island. Occupy the London Stock Exchange made a brief incursion, but the right, helped to their shame by the Church no less, successfully quashed it. St Paul's may be a local 'chapel' but it is of huge symbolic significance, and the Church's failure to answer generously and radically Occupy's question on the cathedral doorstep – what would Jesus do? – set it back decades, while the companies responsible for nearly a decade so far of cruel austerity, with the active help of the Conservatives and the Liberal Democrats, managed to evade punishment or to pay compensatory-level taxes, despite being saved by the taxpayer to breathtaking levels of subsidy.

Jeremy Corbyn's Labour Party is, potentially, another tidal-strength force, one that actually could address the 'poverty, equality and social justice' scandals that weigh the UK down. Perhaps it is not too late: the last gasps of 18 months of Blairite sabotage have subsided and the media bias which Scots warned their English friends about several years ago is that bit more obvious now, and an alternative media is precariously but palpably developing. What is most striking, and most valuable, is that the idea of class bias is back with us, a new dividing line which should unleash much better scrutiny of what lengths the ruling class go to to subdue the energy and life of most of the population.

Richard Price's poetry collections include the award-winning Small World, Lucky Day, *and* Moon for Sale. *A selection of his essays about poetry, small presses and artist's books is collected as* Is This a Poem? *(Molecular Press). He writes here in a personal capacity.*

THE PEOPLE HAVE NOT SPOKEN: DELUSIONS OF THE NEW POPULISM

by Nicholas Murray

Writing about politics – where it is not mere propaganda – generally claims to be an attempt to discover the truth about the world we live in, to offer rational commentary and analysis on public affairs. The underlying assumption is that we can make sense of it all, that there is a coherent logic at work, however irrational or outrageous the principal actors, the politicians, can fitfully make themselves seem. But the language in which this laudable rationality is applied may itself turn out to be more of a problem than we generally concede it to be. If there is a global crisis – of resources, peace, the future of the planet itself – there is also, it seems to me, a crisis of language, of words in the public sphere and what they actually connote.

Orwell's famous 1946 essay 'Politics and the English Language' is the classic embodiment of the view that if only the language can be cleansed, its tools sharpened and oiled for more effective use, then the moral distortions of totalitarian Newspeak, the corruption of political discourse by dishonest words used to express dishonest thoughts, will be replaced by valid truths plainly spoken without the evasive waffle his essay skewered and which has made it a favourite with teachers of good, plain prose ever since – even if some writers have dissented, finding its aesthetic of stripped-down say-what-you-mean insufficiently hospitable to the more creatively disruptive potential of the word.

Orwell, however, was a secular saint, a crystal spirit. The rest of us struggle in a fallen world to make sense of it all even if what we are trying to comprehend often presents itself as senseless. The British general election and its wider context, the argument about how it can forge a new post-European political identity, has obvious connections with the emerging world of Donald Trump, for the driving force behind Brexit was very similar to the negative energy tapped into by Trump: the perceived alienation and disillusion of 'the people', nimbly exploited by the right wing populists who are currently enjoying a great measure of success globally. Indeed the angry male authoritarian – Trump, Erdoğan, Putin, not to mention their long-living peers in other places – is alive and kicking, and often kicking hard. The Arab Spring came and went. Various new popular protest movements like Syriza or Podemos have had their moment but are not currently prevailing. Instead we have the populists and their eager allies in the media.

It would be easy to mock them: the blue-collar workers of the rust belt looking for a saviour in the form of a billionaire property speculator and TV reality show host with not a scrap of political experience, or their British equivalents in the depressed areas of the industrial north turning from the Labour Party to the home counties stockbroker, Nigel Farage. In vain commentators point out that, for example, the people who suffer most from the consequences of climate change denial, a key element of the Trump agenda, are the ones it hurts most. Writing in the *New York Review of Books* last year Nathaniel Rich noted the evidence in Arlie Russell Hochschild's book *Strangers in Their Own Land: Anger and Mourning on the American Right* that in states like Louisiana just such a programme of self-harm was in full swing.

> Across the country, red states are poorer and have more teen mothers, more divorce, worse health, more obesity, more trauma-related deaths, more low-birth-weight babies, and lower school enrolment. On average, people in red states die five years earlier than people in blue states. Indeed, the gap in life expectancy between Louisiana (75.7) and Connecticut (80.8) is the same as that between the United States and Nicaragua.

Our natural impulse is to contest this madness with facts, analysis and rational discourse but in a debating chamber raucous with those infuriating journalistic clichés 'post-truth' or 'fake news' such objective analysis feels beside the point. Politicians like Donald Trump smile and say that the only thing that matters is that he says what his supporters want to hear and what they want to hear is that all their problems are attributable to self-serving capital on East Coast. This is the core of the populist message:

your problems are caused by other people, not yourself, and
we are the only ones listening to you. Trust us, not them.

The populists, who attack 'elites' (while seeming themselves well bedded down in places of privilege) all speak with the same voice. The British popular press, Erdoğan, Trump, concur that the enemy is an independent judiciary, free and critical media, political dissent of the wrong stamp, too much scrutiny of the executive by the legislature, and the dominance of metropolitan intellectual and power elites in the national conversation. If this *were* true, of course, then the populists would have a case, for who would advocate, in a democracy (democracy and populism sharing etymological roots in the notion of the sovereign people) the sidelining, the ignoring, of the people? The traditional answer has been for the people to organise themselves, in trades unions, parties of the working class, radical forms of organisation, community self-help and so forth. This is not what the populists have in mind at all. They are the ones who seek to step forward to speak *for* the people. This is at the core of populism in politics. Their interests would not be served by a genuinely popular insurrection.

There is a flourishing journalistic genre which consists of a reporter catching a train from a main line London station to some provincial outpost, preferably with the right sort of name like Scunthorpe or Hartlepool. It could be written in the office but let's take the trip ourselves. We are met at the station by a taxi which takes us to a community centre where an assembled group of pensioners/unemployed/youth is waiting to be interviewed. The reporter asks why they are disillusioned with the Labour Party (for it will be a part of the country where Labour has been in hegemonic power for decades but is now feeling the pinch from UKIP) and the response will be that not enough has been done to replace the collapsed industries that have closed down or that have been exported to some other country where labour is cheap and conditions of employment significantly worse. There will be a shame-faced reference to Grandma turning in her grave at the thought of her offspring ceasing to vote Labour. 'They're not listening to us,' someone will say on cue and the reporter, instead of asking what it is that they are saying that is not being listened to and what their concrete proposals are for change, will write down the words which are rather similar to those captured by a colleague in her piece 18 months ago, and move on to ask whether they will be voting for UKIP. More shame-faced admissions or perhaps even some defiance and a suggestion that 'because of Brexit' they have little choice but to reject the party whose local representative voted to remain. The taxi-driver will now re-appear and, after a quick whizz around the ravaged town centre (boarded up premises, hairdressers, pound shops, charity shops, Polish delicatessens) to record through the window of the back seat some small brushstrokes of colour (vexingly similar to that earlier colleague's piece) the reporter is dropped off at the station and writes up the article on the laptop before settling into a snooze in first class. It *was* rather an early start.

Somewhere in all this, of course, there are the small glints and gleams of an actual truth. In spite of laughable claims that we are living in a classless society the felt reality for many people in contemporary Britain is that inequalities in income and life chances are rife and it's hardly necessary to line up the statistics that confirm this. It is not just that many people are struggling (when many, palpably, are not) but the precarious gig economy, the teenager catching an expensive bus to the out of town barracks where a hoped for day's zero-hour contracted work turns out, on this particular morning, not to be on offer, the absence of the decent working conditions, pensions, earnings that, fought hard for, were seen in working class communities until recently. Too many of the children of the aristocrats of labour are now working in milord's stables. In the past the unprivileged would organise through trades unions or Labour movement organisations, not wait for the arrival of a billionaire messiah from down south. The certainty that the populists, in spite of their rhetoric, will not deliver on their promises – and can have no serious interest in doing so – is at the core of one's contempt for them.

Facile analogies with the rise of European fascist parties in the 1930s aren't helpful. Trump and Farage, ludicrous as they struggle to make themselves, are not Hitler or Mussolini (though their gratuitous racism is odious and could open the door to more sinister forces), but like those old-time demagogues they know how to use dishonest rhetoric, opportunistically, to advance their own aims. And nothing is more dishonest than their claims to enjoy a popular support that amounts to a rebuke for 'the establishment parties'. A striking fact about the recent triumphs of the authoritarian populists is that they have mostly been elected by a whisker. President Recep Erdoğan won his autocratic powers with 51.4% of the votes at a referendum. Trump won fewer of the popular votes than his rival on similar narrow margins. The Brexit referendum delivered 'victory' to the Leave camp with 51.9% as opposed to 48.1% to remain. And those figures are for the ones who bothered to get out of bed and vote – only 36% of eligible voters entered the polling booth to endorse Brexit. These are hardly landslides, indications of a movement of overwhelming mass support, evidence that, as the Brexiteers put it, 'the people have spoken'. In the British context, as many have pointed out, had the young people who were largely for Remain bothered to cast their votes (only just over a third did) the result would have been very different.

And how did we find ourselves in a situation where a major constitutional or directional change for the future of the country was decided not on the usual basis of a two-thirds majority but on a simple majority of votes? Cultures sceptical of Western plebiscites talk sometimes of the tyranny of the majority. This is very close to being a tyranny of the minority. We should perhaps be grateful that Theresa May, whose Conservative Party has been in government since the last election with fewer than a quarter of the country's votes cast for her party (and who was not even subject to a leadership election within her own organisation) has decided to seek a new mandate. Her conduct in these brief months since she assumed power, her resistance to parliamentary approval of her secret Brexit deals, are not good augurs.

I began by referring to a crisis in the language of politics. By this I meant not just to indict the obvious – the radical disjunction noted above between what people say and what they do (or are likely to do) which is, after all, the stuff of politics, especially where it is dissected in the saloon bar – but something far more intractable. The world of the political scientists, the economists, the sociologists is not the world of the right wing populists. The former, while cordially disagreeing with each other on most issues, share a belief that these issues ought to be debated, evaluated, analysed by rational means using terms that carry at least some referential weight and respectability. The populists, by contrast, and long before the 'post-truth' babble began, operate under different terms of reference. Their values are not the values of established intellectual discourse but an altogether different set of measures of value rooted in visceral promptings, gut instincts, and prejudices interpreted by them to be cherished beliefs that define who people think they are (and who they think they are not). Trying to argue with these notions, that are tenaciously held even if they are hard to engage with on any rational plane, is a considerable challenge. The sense that we find them so will be held by their advocates as a further sign of the gulf between them and those who talk about and analyse politics in official quarters.

This dialogue of the deaf was on display during the British referendum campaign on European Union membership last summer and it will be set up again during the current general election. Never in my lifetime has there been such an ignorant electoral campaign, nor one where the failure of the two sides to even make it look as though they were discussing the same things was so evident. There were in fact two debates going on in parallel and in what looked like parallel universes. The first was a more or less rational debate about whether or not continued membership of the European Union was desirable for Britain. There existed people on both sides of that argument who were capable of conducting it properly. The second was something altogether more elusive, even though its terms were more colourfully presented. Phrases like 'we want to get our country back' were warmly endorsed by the British popular media and replayed back to their constituencies, re-enforcing the message. But what *was* the message? What did this mantra mean? Had any of its chanters actually been to France, Greece, Spain, Italy recently? Is France less French, Greece less Greek than they were before becoming members of the European Union? The answer might be, only in so far as they have been forced to obey the irresistible demands of global capital and its indifference to national boundaries (and national tax rules). *That* form of unelected power over each of our lives was not the subject of any referendum and will never be so, not least because it might be an embarrassment to the owners of the newspapers that shouted most vociferously for Brexit.

Was 'getting our country back' about wresting back power from the European Parliament we had elected or was there a more sinister undertow? A lively *vox pop* on the BBC's *Today* programme in the immediate aftermath of the referendum result captured the voices of a selection of people in Barnsley in Yorkshire, some of whom seemed a little confused about whether the restoration of power had happened overnight and was already operational, all of whom seemed in no doubt that getting our country back was a non-negotiable priority. The BBC has a way of soliciting such voices and plays no small part in defining who is in and who is out of the national breakfast time conversation but, yes, they were real voices and they were not surprising. But behind this phrase another, its dark shadow, flitted. Was the dragon the people had just (by a whisker) slain the invisible 'Brussels bureaucrats' or something else? We were spared that morning as we bit into our toast the phrases 'I'm not racist but…' or 'this is not about immigration' or any of the other variations on that theme which, properly decoded, would be found to mean 'I want to stop immigration by certain groups and not others'. A line was being drawn by people who would normally think of themselves as plain speakers who do not draw lines in what they talk about. Vigorous as the protestations were on all sides that immigration was not the issue – why so vigorous, why protest so much? – it is difficult to believe that it was not the issue.

Whatever the outcome of the current negotiations on withdrawal from the European Union (and regardless of any possible outcome of the current general election in strengthening the authoritarian tendencies of the current Prime Minister in those negotiations) the movement of peoples in the contemporary global economy (not to mention the desperate political refugees whose numbers are unlikely to diminish in the medium term) will continue. There may be some tinkering at the margins but the rest of continental Europe is in no mood to make concessions to English xenophobia and the reality of our economy means that inward migration will not stop. The Barnsley fish and chip shop owner is not going to get everything that he wished for. But he has 'got his country back' and all is well for him.

Personally, I never lost my country and have nothing to retrieve in the new order. It is what it is and, ever since my parents took me as a 14-year-old to stand before Ghiberti's Gates of Paradise on the Baptistery of the Duomo in Florence I have been a European, though admittedly one of the quaint Anglo-Saxon variants. I live in an interconnected world, multi-racial, diverse, endlessly interesting. If it ceases to be so I will not look to some red-faced redneck in a business suit and with an odd hairstyle to lead me to fresher pastures. I will find my own way, thank you. I will not be patronised by populists but I will make my own arrangements and join, if necessary, with people who know how to fight for what they want, as they have always known how to fight, using plain language, and the genuinely popular, tried and tested methods to mount challenges to power.

Nicholas Murray is a poet and literary biographer based in Wales where he runs Rack Press Poetry. His latest verse satire, A Dog's Brexit *has just been published by Melos. He was the winner in 2015 of the Basil Bunting Prize for poetry.*

CONCLUSION: FRANCE AND BEYOND

So, to France: sometimes polls *don't* lie. Though many of the writers in this book are hoping for a moment of refreshing surprise, a malaise has arguably settled over the UK election campaign, and a sense that PM May is now so far ahead, the next weeks will be a sort of pre-victory victory lap. In France, the election of Macron, their youngest-ever President, sends a message to those would-be leaders, like Corbyn, who seemingly ignore polls, and the need for charisma, a strong message of hope, and an ability to use the media positively.

The Corbyn campaign has little of the once-promised momentum (pun sadly intended) – where is the sense of excitement and revolution in the UK we have seen in France? The French have bucked a trend, in electing this untested new dauphin, in one sense, but confirmed another – they did what they had done before, and voted tactically, across parties, to defeat Le Pen. Nigel Farage, and Trump, as well as others, will be disappointed. Their disruptive favourite failed to overcome the ceiling on support for bare-naked hate, now, as recently in the Netherlands.

Europe is not "doing a Brexit" – leading us to ponder the current Anglo-American swing to the far-right as perhaps a more isolated outbreak than was assumed after the shock US election in late 2016.

In speaking to some quite high up in the Labour party, it has become clear they themselves expect to be crushed by a landslide on 8th June. As this book has indicated, the choice is now, for those who do not welcome this outcome, how best to vote, regardless, in the face of near-Beckettian gloom. If at all.

In this sense, a vote for the "anyone but" Tory candidate nearest you, with the best chance of winning, is one tactic; a longer term strategy, as Rosanna Hildyard shows, might be to vote for a more ideal possible future, as with the Greens. If one wants to strengthen Mrs May's hand, of course, one can and will vote Tory. The passion that at times seizes the writers of these articles is impressive, but seems not to have trickled down so much to the electorate – at least not to those not supporting the Conservative swing.

The latest polls, as reported in *The Guardian* on the 7th May (basically with a month to go), are not, in themselves, a cause for complacency, or socialist champagne, but neither do they call for resignation, one would think:

Conservatives	38%
Labour	27%
Lib Dems	18%
UKIP	5%
Others	12%

The Guardian concludes: "May is heading for a majority of 80-100".

Heading? Or already there? It is notable that whereas Macron (in a two person race fair enough) received a resounding 60% and more of the voting public's support, May's 38% is around the level Le Pen has. Only in a first past the post system like ours does 38% actually appear like anything but lukewarm tolerance for hard Brexit.

What do these numbers, if not liars, tell us? UKIP seems finished, more or less, and as Jones has argued, now is simply a sluice to send its toxic message to the Tories. The Lib Dems still have much to play for, and possibly a resurgence of some sort. The SNP now appear to face Ruth Davidson as their chief nemesis, and should do nearly as well as before – but not as resoundingly.

Only Labour really faces its Waterloo – but 11 points behind is not insurmountable, with so many weeks to go. Remember the Canadian election? At this stage, Justin Trudeau was back in third, with numbers lower than Corbyn's. Alas, Corbyn does not do one-armed push-ups and box with his shirt off. His message is not the sunny ways of Trudeau's amazing victory. Rather, the recent plan to pile tax on to earners who earn over £80,000 is already being used by May to show just how old-Labour (Back to the 70s) Corbyn is.

But it is possible, if somewhat unlikely, that if tactical voting, intelligently co-ordinated, takes off over the next weeks and days, then PM May's majority will be a moderately-less-triumphant 60 seats. Still good for her. Brexit won't be stopped, for good or ill. But a devastating mandate might be well-tempered, and in the process, well, who knows what new permutations will emerge, for the post-Brexit landscape – very much another book, to say the least.

Todd Swift
8 May, 2017

EYEWEAR PUBLISHING

EYEWEAR   **JEREMY CORBYN - ACCIDENTAL HERO** W STEPHEN GILBERT
SQUINT   **TRUMP: THE RHETORIC** OLIVER JONES
           THE FRAGILE DEMOCRACY CHRISTOPHER JACKSON

Eyewear Publishing is an independent British small press
dedicated to bringing stylish, affordable, smart books
into the world, ranging from politics to poetry, from
post-punk musicians to prose. Look at what we do at
our website

WWW.EYEWEARPUBLISHING.COM